POSITIVE AFFIRMATIONS
FOR BLACK TEEN BOYS

BUILD CONFIDENCE, STRENGTH, AND KEY HABITS FOR SUCCESS IN SCHOOL, LEADERSHIP, AND WELL-BEING IN 10 MINUTES A DAY

A.C. RODRIGUEZ

CONTENTS

Introduction 7

1. THE POWER OF POSITIVE AFFIRMATIONS 11
   Understand Positive Affirmations and Their
   Impact on the Mind 12
   The Science Behind How Affirmations
   Enhance Self-Perception and Confidence 20
   Crafting Personal Affirmations That Resonate
   With Your Identity and Aspirations 23

2. BUILDING A FOUNDATION OF SELF-
   WORTH AND IDENTITY 31
   Exploring Identity: Connecting With One's
   Roots and Unique Heritage 32
   Affirmations to Strengthen Self-Worth and
   Embrace Individuality Amidst Societal
   Pressures 37
   Reflective Exercises to Uncover Personal
   Values and Strengths 39

3. RESILIENCE AGAINST STEREOTYPES AND
   ADVERSITY 51
   Navigating Stereotypes: Strategies for Teens to
   Maintain a Positive Self-Image 51
   Affirmations and Stories of Resilience to
   Inspire and Build Mental Toughness 56
   Affirmations That Counter Stereotypes and
   Reinforce Inner Strength 61
   Activities to Transform Challenges Into
   Stepping stones for Growth 64

4. CONFIDENCE, LEADERSHIP, AND
COMMUNITY   71
Community Leaders' Crucial Role: Guidance
and Representation   72
Affirmations to Foster Self-Confidence and
Leadership Skills   81
Ideas and Initiatives for Community
Engagement: Developing Leadership Through
Service   83

5. ENVISIONING SUCCESS—ACADEMICS AND
CAREER   93
Affirmations for Academic Motivation and
Envisioning Career Success   94
Setting and Achieving Goals: Strategies for
Academic Excellence and Career Planning   103
Visualization Techniques to Imagine Future
Successes and Create a Roadmap   109

6. CULTIVATING HEALTHY RELATIONSHIPS
AND EFFECTIVE COMMUNICATION   117
The Importance of Healthy Relationships and
Positive Social Circles   118
Exercises to Enhance Communication Skills
and Social Intelligence   127

7. A HOLISTIC APPROACH TO HEALTH AND
WELLNESS   135
Integrating Affirmations With Physical
Wellness   135
Mental and Emotional Health   139
The Art of Mindfulness: Relief and Clarity
Through Mindful Techniques   142
Daily Routines for Wellness   145
Enhancing Motivation Through Enjoyment   148
Weaving Wellness into Daily Life   148

8. PURSUING DREAMS AND SETTING THE
PATH FORWARD   155
Affirmations to Inspire Ambition and the
Pursuit of Dreams   156
Embracing Failures as a Part of Growth   162

Conclusion   173

References   177

INTRODUCTION

Our destinies are our own to shape. The sooner we learn, understand, and believe this, the sooner we can build lives that match our visions. But it can be challenging. As we explore our world, we find old and new limits designed to slow us down or even stop us altogether. Many of these limits target specific groups based on age, gender, sexual preference, or race. It can make you feel trapped, forced to hide parts of yourself, or downplay your strengths. The pressure can be overwhelming. Why try when it feels like you'll never be enough, like they'll never fully accept you?

The experience of a young Black man is uniquely challenging. You might feel like your destiny was decided at birth, shaped entirely by the color of your skin, well before anyone knows your mind or heart. People judge you, sometimes harshly, from the moment they see you. Teachers, employers, strangers on the street—the whispers, stares, and subtle avoidance starts young. Those experiences can really hurt.

I know. I've been there. I heard those doubts every day from peers and coworkers, even those with "good" intentions. As a soldier, I learned that society could reduce me to a stereotype, a distraction.

But they were wrong. I'm living proof that being Black doesn't define your limits. Most young Black men fight a more challenging battle than I ever did on a literal battlefield. You struggle with your identity in a world that doesn't want to understand or accept it. Loudly and subtly, others tell you that you're "less than" as you grapple with your own doubts. These voices chip away at your confidence, hope, and vision of a happy, prosperous future.

You may try to fit in, soften your voice, and separate from your roots. Maybe you lash out in anger. Perhaps you've started to believe those lies—that happiness and success aren't meant for you. It breaks my heart because I've been there. Then, I discovered the power of positive affirmations.

They were my weapons—not against enemies, but against the voices inside my head. By choosing how I spoke to myself, I changed the course of my life. Affirmations fueled my determination, cut through self-doubt, and showed me a path where being Black was a strength, not a limitation.

You want to do more than survive. You want to thrive, conquer the voices inside and out, and build a life where you're proud of who you are while achieving your biggest dreams. This book gives you the tools I wish I'd had as a confused, scared teen. With it, you'll discover:

- How to armor yourself against hurtful words and negativity—not with silence but with inner strength.
- How do you find acceptance and love for yourself? It all starts within.
- Ways to ignite unshakeable self-belief—a fire brighter than any discrimination.
- The roadmap to set goals and achieve them proves to yourself and everyone else that you're unstoppable.

These aren't just promises. I've lived it. Our heroes prove it, from Jackie Robinson breaking barriers in baseball to Barack Obama ascending to the world's most powerful office. Imagine your anxieties replaced by a sense of peace about who you are. Fear of rejection is drowned out by your confidence to be your true self. That energy powers your ambitions, leading you to find your people, your purpose, and a future brighter than you ever imagined.

Here are a few successful Black people who harnessed the power of affirmations and self-belief (Williams, 2015):

Oprah Winfrey

The media mogul's journey from poverty to becoming one of the wealthiest women on the planet underscores the power of positive thinking. Oprah Winfrey's resilience started young: Watching her grandmother toil, she repeatedly affirmed to herself, "My life won't be like this. My life will be better." This mantra of hope and determination laid the groundwork for her extraordinary life and career, showcasing the profound impact of nurturing a vision of a better future.

Will Smith

Another staunch advocate of the law of attraction is Will Smith, whose career is a testament to the power of positive thinking. Smith once said, "In my mind, I've always been an A-list Hollywood superstar. Y'all just didn't know yet." His success is attributed to his visualization and belief in his capabilities, consistently aligning with the wise words of Confucius: "He who says he can and he who says he can't are both usually right."

It will be challenging. But every day you fight for a positive mindset is a victory. Those victories add up. As a soldier who's faced death, I promise you that this fight is the most important one you'll ever win.

Let's get started.

THE POWER OF POSITIVE AFFIRMATIONS

Imagine someone you admire's greatest accomplishment, such as hitting their record-earning home run, discovering a scientific breakthrough, or getting their dream job. Now, picture the doubt and denial that came along with accomplishing it, and consider how much easier the task would have been if all those negative thoughts, or even half of them, had been positive. Often, when we strive for personal success, we unintentionally turn into our own worst adversaries, only realizing this after completing the task. No matter how much support you have from family or friends, you'll usually find that words of encouragement have their limitations. A critical factor in achieving success is nurturing a mindset that instills confidence and passion, supported by a personalized, internalized support system. However, nature does not naturally wire our brains to provide this kind of support. We need to act to train our minds to think in this way.

UNDERSTAND POSITIVE AFFIRMATIONS AND THEIR IMPACT ON THE MIND

Positive affirmations are powerful statements that can help you challenge negativity and develop a more hopeful outlook. They act as mental codes, allowing you to achieve success in your mind. Affirmations are like gym exercises for your confidence and self-belief. Regularly reciting positive statements, phrases, or words can change your thinking about yourself and what you do. Your brain associates these positive words with pleasurable experiences, activating reward areas and reducing stress or pain. We use affirmations to manifest goals, overcome challenges, and boost self-confidence. When you repeatedly recite them, your brain can permanently change its thinking patterns. You may naturally feel skeptical if you're new to this practice, so let's address that first.

Skepticism is natural when it comes to trying out new practices, especially ones that involve changing your mindset. However, it's important to approach affirmations with an open mind and give them a fair chance. Scientific research has shown that positive affirmations can significantly impact our well-being and success.

You might not know it, but your mind is more incredible than that of the most advanced supercomputer. It's constantly changing and adapting, influenced by everything you see, hear, and think. The more you dwell on something, the stronger its connection gets in your brain. That's awesome when it's positive thoughts, but it can backfire when negativity takes the lead.

As a young Black man, you've probably absorbed a ton of harmful messages designed to limit your potential. Those whispers from teachers, those stares filled with judgment, those stereotypes you see in movies—all of that sinks in, whether you want it to or not. Over time, they can mess with your sense of self and make it hard to see your own brilliance.

This is where affirmations become your secret weapon. They tap into a concept researchers call self-affirmation theory. Basically, we all have this deep-down need to see ourselves as good, capable, and worthy. When we tell ourselves positive things, it activates our brain's reward system. We feel a sense of calm and confidence—almost like a hit of good vibes.

Here's the science: Every thought triggers a whole chain reaction in your body. Neurotransmitters, those chemical messengers, start firing, impacting everything from your mood to your physical health. The more often you repeat something (even silently to yourself), the stronger those brain pathways become. Scientists have seen how repeated affirmations stimulate specific brain regions linked to positive thinking and self-worth. Indeed, research supports the concept that affirming our beliefs in a positive manner can help sustain our self-integrity. Moore (2019) notes that there are empirical studies confirming that self-affirmations can effectively bolster our sense of self and reinforce our core values.

Affirmations are like training wheels for your confidence. At first, it might feel weird or awkward to say good things about yourself. But the more you practice, the more natural it feels. You're literally rewiring your brain to believe in the good stuff and pushing back against the negativity that's been trying to take root.

How Affirmations Strengthen Your Identity: Self-identity is all about defining who you are deep down inside. That includes your strengths, your values, and your dreams. Affirmations help you break free from the labels and limitations others may try to put on you. You decide how you see yourself, and affirmations give you the tools to make that positive vision stronger and clearer each day.

Benefits: Think of those people you admire who handle challenges like champs and never seem to lose their cool. Affirmations can help you develop similar mental toughness. Studies have shown they can:

- **Bust stress:** Lowering stress isn't just about feeling good; it boosts your physical health too!
- **Motivate action:** When you believe in yourself, you're more likely to go for it, whether it's studying harder or trying something new.
- **Build resilience:** Affirmations help you bounce back from tough times, reminding you of your worth when others try to bring you down.
- **Promote a healthier outlook:** Positive thinking can improve your well-being and influence positive health behaviors.

Remember, change takes time and practice. Be patient with yourself. But know that each time you speak an affirmation with belief, you're creating a powerful shift in your mind.

That's how you take control of your thoughts and build a rock-solid foundation of self-belief that no one can shake.

The Power of Language: Culture, Identity, and Growth

Language is more than just words; it reflects your culture, its history, and how you see the world—including yourself. As noted by Zagada (2020), anthropological linguist Daniel Everett posits that language functions as a cultural tool, reflecting and shaping the values and ideals of a community over time. As a young Black man, the way you speak holds a unique power born from a rich and complex history.

The Resilience of Black Language and Culture: African American language and culture have roots that run deep. The horrors of slavery brought individuals from diverse African tribes together. Yet, they didn't lose their voice. Instead, they forged a unique way of communicating, blending elements of various African languages with the English their oppressors imposed. This spirit of resilience continued to thrive through movements like the Harlem Renaissance, where Black art and literature amplified the beauty and power of Black expression.

Your slang, phrases, and rhythm are more than just words; they are a powerful inheritance. They are echoes of your ancestors' ability to find joy and connection even in the darkest of times. Unfortunately, there are those who fear or misunderstand your power and attempt to use your language against you. But remember, your voice is not a weakness but a strength. You have the power to wield it, to elevate yourself and those around you, and to combat the negativity that may surround you. Your voice is your armor, your shield, and your sword.

Language shapes perception: How we speak directly impacts how we think, both about the world and ourselves. That's why it's so important to become conscious of the words you choose. This doesn't mean giving up who you are; it means learning to grow and evolve the way you speak, both to express yourself fully and to change the inner dialogue that can hold you back.

Elevating Your Language: This doesn't mean always talking super "proper." It's about becoming a language chameleon. Knowing when to speak with the fire and flow of your community and when to adapt your style to unlock new connections and opportunities. It's about replacing the negativity you may have overheard (or even told yourself) with words that build you up and fuel your ambition. Adapting your language is not a betrayal of your roots but a way to expand your horizons and embrace new possibilities.

Your language is not just a reflection of your cultural pride but also a powerful catalyst for personal growth and empowerment. Its essence is symbolic of who you are, where you are from, and what you represent, while its growth or evolution is an indicator of your own and can make you an overall better and more effective communicator. So what does this mean? Embrace your roots, understanding the power and potential they hold. But also, don't be afraid to evolve your language to adapt it to new situations and opportunities. By becoming more conscious of the words you use—outwardly and within your own mind—you shape your perspective and pave the way for the amazing future you're going to create.

Use this information to shape how you communicate with the world and, more importantly, how you communicate with yourself.

What Is a Fixed Mindset?

We all make mistakes and fall short of our goals. Sometimes, we even let people down, including ourselves. However, what truly matters is how we respond to those challenging moments. Do we tell ourselves that we are failures or question our worth, thinking we will never be good enough? If these thoughts sound familiar, then we are experiencing what psychologists call a fixed mindset. A fixed mindset is like having a bully trapped inside your head. It leads you to believe that your abilities, intelligence, and even your worth as a person are fixed and unchanging. It convinces you that failure is permanent, not a step on the road to something better. This toxic way of thinking is one of the biggest obstacles you can face in life.

Now, here's something you need to understand: A fixed mindset can sneak up on anyone, regardless of how strong your support system may be. But as a young Black man, there are forces in the world actively trying to push you into that trap. They want you to believe lies about what you can and can't do because of the color of your skin. Don't let those lies take root.

Understanding how a fixed mindset operates is the first step to breaking free from its limitations. It's natural to get discouraged at times. But don't confuse a momentary setback with who you are and where you're going. You can shut down the fixed mindset voice and replace it with a mindset that will help you succeed faster the sooner you recognize it.

What Is a Growth Mindset?

Remember that bully voice we talked about, the one trapped in your head? The good news is that you can beat the bully. That's when having a mindset focused on growth becomes important. It's a way of thinking that turns failures into fuel. The foundation of a growth mindset is the unwavering belief that there is never a limit to improvement and growth. Think of your brain as a muscle. Does a weightlifter get strong after one gym session? Not likely. But with consistent effort, they get stronger with each workout. Your brain works the same way—the challenges you tackle and the mistakes you learn from all of them help you become smarter, more resilient, and more powerful.

With a growth mindset, instead of saying, "I can't," you ask, "How can I learn?". Instead of giving up, you get curious: "What could I try differently?" It's about believing in your ability to learn and improve, knowing that each attempt, even if imperfect, gets you one step closer to your goal.

This mindset is especially important for young Black men. The world may try to throw obstacles at you and tell you that you can't succeed because of how you look or where you're from. A growth mindset is your armor against those lies. It's knowing that your future is limitless, defined by your determination and not anyone else's limits. It's not enough to just want to succeed. To overcome challenges and reach your full potential, you need a mindset. It's about embracing the journey and knowing that every step, even the difficult ones, is getting you closer to becoming the best version of yourself.

Fixed vs. Growth Mindset in Action

Let's see how these two mindsets play out in everyday situations:

Example 1: Learning Guitar

- **Fixed Mindset:** "I suck at music. I'll never figure this guitar out. See, I'm just not talented like other people."
- **Growth Mindset:** "Learning anything new takes time. Everyone learns at their own pace. I'll get better with practice."
- **Affirmations:** "I am patient with myself as I learn." "My skills grow stronger every day."

Example 2: Learning a New Language

- **Fixed Mindset:** "Language classes are too hard. I'm not a 'language person.' This is pointless."
- **Growth Mindset:** "This is challenging, but it'll open up a whole new world. I might struggle now, but I'll keep at it."
- **Affirmations:** "My mind is capable of amazing things." "I embrace new ways of communicating."

Example 3: Joining the Debate Team

- **Fixed Mindset:** "Those kids are way smarter than me. I'd embarrass myself. I'm not good at public speaking."
- **Growth Mindset:** "Debating seems exciting but a little scary. I bet I could learn a lot, even if I don't become a star right away."
- **Affirmations:** "My voice deserves to be heard." "I find strength in every challenge."

Example 4: Asking Someone Out

- **Fixed Mindset:** "She'd never say yes. What if she laughs at me? I'm better off not even trying."
- **Growth Mindset:** "Rejection is part of life. I won't know unless I try. If I don't ask, the answer is always no."
- **Affirmations:** "I am worthy of love and connection." "I am confident and courageous."

It's OK to feel the fear or doubt that comes with a fixed mindset. However, the growth mindset is about recognizing those thoughts and then choosing the braver option anyway. Affirmations will help you make that courageous choice.

THE SCIENCE BEHIND HOW AFFIRMATIONS ENHANCE SELF-PERCEPTION AND CONFIDENCE

In a study that aimed to explore the neural basis of self-affirmation, researchers discovered that individuals who engaged in self-affirmation displayed increased activity in brain areas that are involved in self-reflection and valuation. These areas encompass the medial prefrontal cortex and posterior cingulate cortex, associated with self-processing, as well as the ventral striatum and ventral medial prefrontal cortex, linked to value assessment. The enhanced brain activity was more noticeable when participants thought about their core values oriented towards the future rather than their daily activities (Cascio et al., 2015).

Your mind is more powerful than you might think! Positive affirmations—those short, empowering statements you say to yourself—actually change the way your brain works. They light up your brain's reward centers, such as when you win at your favorite video game or eat good food. This builds up neural pathways for positive thinking and confidence. Bottom line: affirmations can help you feel better AND unlock your potential.

But it's not just about happy thoughts. Science shows how affirmations can:

- **Breaking down your stress:** Stress isn't just a feeling; it affects your body. Affirmations can help lower unhealthy stress levels.
- **Build healthy habits:** Affirmations can motivate you to exercise, make smarter choices, and stick to your goals.
- **Boost learning:** They can prime your brain for taking in new info, making studying more effective.

Beware of Brain Tricks

Your brain is amazing, but it's got some quirks we ALL need to watch out for:

- **The "Expert" Trap:** Sometimes, when you're new at something, you think you're better than you are, and when you're really good, you underestimate yourself. It's weird but true! Don't get too cocky or too discouraged; keep learning.
- **The "Everywhere" Illusion:** You notice something new, like a song or a type of car, and suddenly, it seems to be ALL OVER. Your brain is just paying more attention now; it doesn't mean the world has changed.
- **The Belief Bubble:** Ever wonder why people get so heated about things you disagree with? Our brains favor information that supports what we already believe. Affirmations can help you stay more open-minded and learn from everyone.

Your brain is always adapting. You're not stuck with negative thoughts or bad habits. Using affirmations can be a potent technique for changing the way you think, but it's equally vital to understand your thought process to become a more optimistic and self-assured individual.

CRAFTING PERSONAL AFFIRMATIONS THAT RESONATE WITH YOUR IDENTITY AND ASPIRATIONS

Your affirmations are like your personal theme songs or slogans that help you stay motivated. They don't have to be unique or creative. Even generic affirmations can be super helpful in getting you started. However, to feel the full effects and make them stand out, you should personalize your affirmations to speak directly to your challenges, goals, and dreams. You should also ensure that they are written and recited in a tone, voice, and language that speak to you personally. Since you are the only one who will hear them, don't hold back on how unique or elaborate you make the wording. You can even incorporate your own jargon or slang. The primary consideration to remember when writing or rewriting your personal affirmations is effectiveness. You should ensure they leave the mark you want and need them to leave in your mind.

Unlocking the Power of Personalized Affirmations

Here are a few points to help you create powerful personalized affirmations:

- **Ownership:** When you repeat affirmations, you take ownership of your beliefs and perceptions about yourself. It's a way of consciously shaping your thoughts and programming your mind to align with your true identity and potential. By stating affirmations, you are actively telling your brain what you believe about yourself, reinforcing positive beliefs, and letting go of negative self-perceptions.

- **Authenticity:** Affirmations that reflect your personality, values, and individuality have a much deeper impact. When you use affirmations that resonate with who you truly are, they become more meaningful and powerful. Generic affirmations may not connect with you on a personal level, but when you craft affirmations that align with your authentic self, they can ignite a sense of purpose and motivation within you.

- **Cultural Connection:** As a young Black man, incorporating affirmations that draw strength from your heritage can be empowering. Affirmations that speak your community's language acknowledge your cultural roots and celebrate their strengths and resilience, providing a sense of belonging and connection. They can serve as a reminder of the rich history and legacy that you come from, inspiring you to embrace your identity and overcome any challenges that may come your way.

- **Goal Alignment:** When you focus your affirmations on what you genuinely want to achieve, you are aligning your thoughts and intentions with your goals. Affirmations can help you visualize and manifest your dreams into reality. You are programming your subconscious mind to work towards those goals by consistently affirming your desires and aspirations. This alignment between your affirmations and goals creates a powerful synergy that propels you toward success and fulfillment.

Building Your Affirmations

Here's a step-by-step process to get those custom affirmations flowing. Use these points as inspiration to picture the person you want to be in the future and the changes you want these affirmations to bring forth. Please write down your thoughts or answers for each point as you read them. These notes will help you write your affirmations in the next steps:

1. **Your Future:** Picture yourself not as you are now but ten years from now. What have you achieved? How do you feel? Let yourself imagine it!
2. **The Highlights Reel:** Write a few highlights from your future life. These could be big (I'm the CEO of my company) or personal (I'm a role model to my younger siblings).
3. **What's Your Superpower?** Identify a trait, talent, or value that runs through your vision. It could be creativity, leadership, or perseverance.
4. **Turn it into an Affirmation**. Start with "I am..." or "I have..." and add your strength and goal. Example: "I am a visionary leader creating positive change in my community."

Examples to Spark Your Creativity

Get inspired by these, but then tweak them to make them uniquely yours:

- **Overcoming Toxic Relationships:** "I walk away from negativity." "I choose friends who bring out my best."
- **Self-Respect:** "My voice matters." "My ancestors' strength flows through me."
- **Positive Outlook:** "I find joy in every day."

How to Write Your Affirmations

Keep these tips in mind while creating your power statements:

- **Present Tense:** "I am..." not "I will be..."
- **Positive Vibes:** Focus on what you do want.
- **Grounded but Bold:** Believable yet ambitious.
- **Your Truth:** Reflects your inner strengths.
- **Just a Few to Start:** Pick those that resonate most. You can always add new ones.

Affirmation Creation Worksheet

Let's get to finding your purpose and crafting your path to drive it. We've provided an Affirmation Creation Worksheet to get you going on your journey. Follow the prompts, be open and honest with yourself, and you'll soon have crafted your own personal affirmations.

Affirmation Creation Worksheet

State your obstacle or improvement. Write what you wish to accomplish/overcome.

Example: "I want to have more confidence at work/school." "My _____ is toxic."

1.

2.

3.

Write your power words. Choose words or traits you're proud of or want to develop.

Examples: Honesty, Commitment, Adaptability, Humbleness, Logical, can let go.

Write what you need to overcome/improve and how your power traits can aid you in it.

Example: Confidence personal value, logic /Toxic friend- able to let go, honest

1.

2.

3.

Craft your affirmations.

Example:

Goal: Confidence at Work.

Affirmations:

1. I know my value; my logic makes me an asset.
2. I am a proud member of the Black community; I hold my head high among my peers.

Goal: Dealing with Toxic Friends

Affirmations:

1. I choose to remove toxic relationships from my life.
2. I don't let toxicity linger; I keep my mind free of distractions.

Goal:

Affirmations:

1.

2.

3.

Goal:

Affirmations:

1.

2.

3.

Goal:

Affirmations:

1.

2.

Final Thoughts

Remember, affirmations aren't just a nice idea; science shows they can literally change the way your brain works. Building a positive mindset isn't magic; it's about training your brain to focus on what empowers you. Personalize them and make them resonate with your own experiences and aspirations. Reflect on your values, goals, and the person you want to become. Don't just adopt someone else's slogans or generic affirmations. Invest time in crafting affirmations that align with your unique journey. Think about the qualities and attributes you admire in yourself. Visualize the amazing person you aspire to be. Use these reflections as a foundation for your affirmations. For example, if you value kindness, create an affirmation like, "I am a compassionate person who spreads love and positivity wherever I go."

Remember, affirmations should be an ongoing conversation with yourself. Let them evolve and grow as you do. As you progress on your personal development journey, you may discover new aspects of yourself that you want to cultivate or different goals you want to achieve. Continuously revisit and revise your affirmations to keep them relevant and inspiring. Crafting affirmations takes time, so be patient and allow room for self-discovery. Embrace the journey of becoming the amazing person you envision. Let your affirmations guide and remind you of the incredible potential within you.

Now that you're harnessing the power of affirmations, it's time to go deeper. In the next chapter, we'll tackle another major key to success: building an unshakeable foundation of self-worth and identity. This is how you'll navigate challenging relationships, break free from any limits others try to put on you, and step fully into your own power. Get ready to discover your strength and build a future of limitless potential!

BUILDING A FOUNDATION OF
SELF-WORTH AND IDENTITY

B iologically speaking, we are all made up of the same building blocks. Whether you are an All-State Linebacker or a budding Thespian, what makes you a person is not different from what makes me a person. But what makes you, you?

This is a question as old as constructive thinking itself. Some of the greatest Philosophical minds of all time have devoted countless hours to pondering and arguing about what makes us individuals. So why shouldn't we spend a few minutes of our time asking ourselves the same question? We all have different backgrounds and different starting points in life, but we all have the necessary ingredients to bounce back from any adversary. We are resilient people. What separates those who are at the top of their field from those who are not is how they play the cards they are dealt.

EXPLORING IDENTITY: CONNECTING WITH ONE'S ROOTS AND UNIQUE HERITAGE

A history that extends far beyond our own lifetime shapes each and every one of us. Like a tree with deep roots, our identities are connected to those of our ancestors. We draw strength from their stories and the values they passed down. These roots, filled with the names we carry, blood in our veins, strengths, and struggles, might stretch across continents or through times we don't even remember. They all shape who we are, influencing everything from our traditions to how we see the world. Even small things, like knowing your great-grandma's favorite recipe, can be a powerful link to your past. Your cultural legacy, unique to your family, makes your story unlike anyone else's.

Grasping the essence of your cultural and familial heritage is a bridge to a broader community that stretches across generations and, more often than not, spans the globe. This journey towards understanding is not only a marker of maturity but also a profound expression of self-respect. It fosters a sense of pride within and projects an image of strength and wisdom to the wider world. Embracing your heritage may take various forms—be it learning the language of your ancestors, partaking in their traditions, or upholding their values. However, the mere act of recognizing and valuing these aspects of your identity is a significant step towards self-definition.

As a member of the black community, it is critical that you acknowledge the entirety of your history, embracing both its triumphs and tribulations. In a world where some may seek to obscure their cultural roots or distort historical truths for personal gain or societal standing, recognizing the full breadth of your heritage is an act of resistance and empowerment. It's essential to resist following in the footsteps of those who have historically sought to suppress diverse cultures, including your own. By honoring your history and heritage, you assert your place in the world and challenge the narratives imposed by those aiming to preserve a skewed hierarchy.

Heritage is not merely a reflection of the past; it serves as a lens through which people view themselves, their ancestors, and their contemporaries, and it influences how they interact with the world around them today (Kurin, 2022). Remember, understanding your heritage connects you not only to the past but also to a collective strength and wisdom that propels you forward. It's about more than just personal identity; it's about belonging to a lineage that has endured, thrived, and contributed to the tapestry of human experience. This acknowledgment and celebration of your roots empowers you to navigate the world with confidence, grounded in your knowledge of who you are and the legacy you carry.

Why Your Heritage Matters:

- **Resilience:** Knowing your family's history shows you what people who share your bloodline have overcome. That knowledge fuels your own inner strength.
- **Community:** Embracing your heritage connects you to a larger community than yourself. It's a reminder that you're never alone.

- **Pride:** As a young Black man, parts of your heritage might include painful chapters. But it also holds stories of courage, creativity, and the unbroken spirit of your ancestors. You carry that legacy.

Taking Action:

- **Family Tree:** Even a basic one with names and birthdates helps you visualize your heritage.
- **Explore Your Roots:** If you have access to family stories and information, that's amazing! Start there. If not, exploring the African diaspora's broader history and culture is just as powerful. It gives you a sense of belonging and connection that's vital to your identity.
- **Talk it Out:** If older relatives are willing to share, listen to their stories. But you can also talk with friends, mentors, or even community leaders about their experiences and what their heritage means to them.
- **Ignite Your Curiosity:** Learn about Black historical figures, important cultural movements, and the diverse communities within the Black experience. Seek out books, documentaries, websites, and even local cultural events.

History and Heritage: Heroes Who Embrace Their Blackness

Many individuals, including artists, political leaders, inventors, innovators, and activists, have paved the way for your unique journey. These figures, in the face of adversity, embraced their culture and heritage with unwavering pride despite facing disparagement, abuse, and discouragement. Their resilience and dedication serve as a beacon, illuminating the way for others. Here, we highlight a few of these remarkable individuals whose lives and legacies offer inspiration and encouragement in exploring your history and heritage.

Langston Hughes

Langston Hughes was a cornerstone of the Harlem Renaissance, using his pen to weave the tapestry of African American life into the fabric of American literature. His poetry and writing celebrated black culture and identity, often addressing social injustices and the complexity of the black experience in America. Hughes embraced his blackness by vividly portraying the joys, struggles, and indomitable spirit of his people, inspiring generations to take pride in their heritage.

Harriet Jacobs

Harriet Jacobs, an escaped slave, became an influential abolitionist, author, and reformer. Her autobiography, "Incidents in the Life of a Slave Girl," penned under the pseudonym Linda Brent, delved into the sexual harassment and abuse faced by enslaved women, offering a groundbreaking perspective on the atrocities of slavery. Jacobs' brave decision to publicly share her experiences was an act of defiance against the oppressive system of slavery, emphasizing the resilience and dignity of black women.

Jackie Robinson

1947 marked a pivotal moment in baseball history as Jackie Robinson became the first African American player to jump the color barrier in the major leagues. Intense racial discrimination and hostility marked his entry into baseball. Yet, Robinson's exceptional skill, dignity, and perseverance in the face of such adversity challenged the deeply entrenched racial prejudices of the time, paving the way for future generations of athletes of all backgrounds.

Barack Obama

Barack Obama's presidency as the 44th President of the United States was a historic moment in American history, as he shattered historical barriers by becoming the first African American to hold the position. His presidency symbolized a milestone in the long journey toward equality and recognition of black excellence in the highest echelons of political power. Obama embraced his multicultural heritage and blackness with pride, often speaking candidly about the challenges and biases he faced. His leadership and achievements demonstrated the potential for black individuals to effect significant change on a global stage, serving as a profound inspiration for young people everywhere.

Each of these figures, in their own unique way, embraced their identity and heritage to make indelible marks on history. Their stories of resilience, courage, and achievement in the face of adversity provide powerful motivation for black teens to embrace their own heritage and identity as sources of strength and pride.

AFFIRMATIONS TO STRENGTHEN SELF-WORTH AND EMBRACE INDIVIDUALITY AMIDST SOCIETAL PRESSURES

When recited consistently, affirmations can imbue you with a profound sense of self-worth and autonomy, empowering you to stride forward with pride and your head held high. Customizing these affirmations to echo your unique culture and the traditions, customs, and values passed down from your ancestors becomes particularly empowering when you might feel isolated or uneasy, immersed in an environment dominated by cultures different from your own. All backgrounds share these universal human experiences. The goal is to navigate confidently amongst diverse cultures, fully engaging with them while also feeling wholly at ease with your own identity. Affirmations serve as a supportive tool in achieving this balance.

Let's look at a few that you can use or reword into your own:

- I am a proud descendant of strength, resilience, and wisdom. My heritage empowers me to face any challenge with grace.
- The legacy of my ancestors fuels my journey. I carry their dreams and achievements as a badge of honor.
- I embrace the beauty of my culture, letting it shine through me in all environments. My uniqueness is my strength.
- My voice carries the echoes of my ancestors. It speaks truths rooted in a rich heritage that guides my way.

- In my veins flows the courage of warriors, the wisdom of sages, and the hope of dreamers. I am the future they envisioned.
- Every day, I embrace my identity, understanding that my uniqueness is a mosaic of various cultural influences.
- My skin is a map of journeys, stories, and triumphs. It carries the legacy of heroes who walked before me.
- I am a beacon of my culture's light and warmth, shining brightly in any setting. My heritage is my compass.
- My uniqueness is my superpower. I navigate diverse cultures with empathy and understanding, always true to myself.
- I honor my past by forging my path with determination and pride. My heritage is the wind beneath my wings.
- I draw strength from my roots. They bind me to my values and propel me forward with confidence.

Recite these affirmations daily or adapt them to better suit your personal story and the specifics of your cultural heritage. Remember, affirmations are most effective when they feel deeply personal and resonate with your innermost beliefs about yourself and your place in the world. However, please note that these affirmations are general in nature and may not resonate with everyone. By integrating these affirmations into your everyday schedule, you enhance your self-value and embrace your distinctiveness, preparing yourself to flourish amid societal pressures.

REFLECTIVE EXERCISES TO UNCOVER PERSONAL VALUES AND STRENGTHS

Reflection, a fundamental pillar of mental well-being, is a personal journey that offers a straightforward yet enlightening practice. It can provide profound insights into your unique identity and avenues for self-improvement. The beauty of reflection lies in its simplicity; all that's required is your willingness to engage in self-examination. Reflection involves taking a step back to objectively consider your actions and the actions of those around you, akin to analyzing your life's narrative to understand the motivations behind your choices and experiences. This process of introspection can be as beneficial as therapy or mentoring when approached with sincerity and openness. In this section, we will explore several exercises aimed at helping you identify your core values and strengths. Similar to the affirmations you've crafted for yourself, these exercises tailor to your journey, emphasizing the uniqueness of each individual's self-discovery journey. The outcomes of these exercises are invaluable in shaping your path forward, whether through positive change or by affirming the positive aspects of your life.

Exercise 1: Relax and Reflect

This exercise is a gentle introduction to introspection. It invites you to pause and look back on a moment from your recent past—it could be a significant event, a memory that lingered in your mind, or even the simple beginnings of your day at school this week. The aim is to:

1. **Select Your Moment:** Choose a specific event or moment to focus on. It doesn't have to be monumental; even the mundane can offer rich insights.
2. **Engage Your Senses:** Recall what you saw, heard, felt, tasted, or smelled during this moment. Engaging your senses can bring the memory to life and offer a deeper understanding of your experience.
3. **Identify Your Feelings:** Reflect on the emotions you experienced during this moment. Were you excited? Anxious? Joyful? Reflecting on our emotional responses can give us clues about our values and preferences.
4. **Consider the Impact:** Consider how this moment has affected your day or your week. Did it affect your mood, influence your decisions, or change your perspective?
5. **Draw a Lesson:** Identify a lesson or takeaway from this moment. It may have revealed something about your personality, relationships, or environment.

This reflective practice is not just about reminiscence; it's an opportunity to cultivate mindfulness and gain insight into your journey. Regularly engaging in this simple exercise can enhance your awareness of the present and help you develop a deeper connection with your inner self.

Exercise 2: Self-Q & A

While echoing the practice of affirming one's self, this exercise shifts the focus towards introspection to uncover current and historical motivations. These questions deepen your understanding of yourself, exploring what you deem significant or value most. Even if you believe you know yourself well, it's essential to recognize that personality, like all aspects of life, is layered and complex, often revealing new facets over time. For instance, your affinity for lasagna might have originated from its similarity to pizza in your youth, but as you matured, you discovered a deeper appreciation for the interplay of its ingredients, such as the creamy mozzarella and tangy meat sauce.

Here are a few reflective questions to guide your journey of self-discovery:

- What principles hold the most importance to me?
- How would I describe a perfect day, and what underlying values does this reflect?
- What activities do I choose to spend my free time doing?
- What are the pursuits that bring me joy?
- If there were no constraints, what would I choose to do with my life?

These questions invite you to explore the core of your being, revealing the motivations and passions that propel your existence. This self-dialogue is a step toward recognizing and embracing the multifaceted nature of your personality and values.

Exercise 3: Core Values Discovery Through Selection and Categorization

In this engaging activity, you'll embark on a quest to identify five core values that are intrinsically tied to your identity, utilizing a systematic narrowing-down process. This exercise perfectly suits a collaborative effort with friends or family, providing a fun and insightful way to uncover more about each other's values and principles. Here's how to dive in:

1. Choose the values that are important to you from the list provided below and write them down.

passion	affection	prosperity	flexibility	foresight
confidence	gratitude	consideration	collaboration	achievement
heritage	distinctiveness	consistency	clarity	alertness
duty	discipline	inventiveness	expertise	initiative
readiness	influence	fame	recreation	flawlessness
spirit	solidarity	daring	excellence	execution
novelty	openness	hope	drive	education
insight	perception	creativity	originality	inclusion
adaptability	justice	compassion	bravery	uniformity

2. Group your chosen values into categories that make sense to you, with a maximum of five groupings. For example, if you've picked flexibility and open-mindedness, you might group them together because they both relate to change.

3. Select one value from each group that serves as an overall label for the group, or create a label if no value stands out.

4. You can choose to stop the exercise here or add a verb to each core value to make it actionable.

5. Order the core values from most important to least important to challenge yourself and write the prioritized list.

Exercise 4: Friends and Family Reflection and Insights

This exercise taps into the perspectives of those who know you best—your friends and family—to offer you a mirror reflecting the best aspects of yourself, sometimes those you might overlook. Here's how to embark on this insightful journey:

Step 1: Select Your Circle

Compile a list of close friends and family members. Choose individuals who have witnessed the spectrum of your experiences, from triumphant highs to challenging lows, and whose honesty you value. Aim for a diverse group that includes people from various segments of your life—those you live with, schoolmates, teammates, and individuals from both your past and present.

Step 2: Personal Outreach

Reach out to each person individually with a request for reflection. Personalized communication fosters sincerity and increases the likelihood of thoughtful responses. Ask them to think of a moment when they saw you at your best. Ensure the request is straightforward and uniform across all your inquiries to maintain consistency in the feedback you receive.

Step 3: Analyze the Feedback

Once you've gathered the responses, look for recurring themes or traits that stand out. Organizing the feedback into a chart may help you visualize patterns and pinpoint who observed what qualities. This analytical step is crucial for identifying the strengths and positive attributes recognized by your community.

Step 4: Create Your Self-Identity Map

Synthesize the gathered insights into a self-identity map or chart. This visualization should encapsulate the qualities and moments where you shine brightest, as seen through the eyes of those who care about you. This map serves as a testament to your strengths and the positive impact you have on those around you.

Step 5: Leverage Your Strengths

Use your self-identity map as a guide to enhance your life. If specific situations or talents consistently highlight your best self, seek opportunities to engage in them more frequently. Additionally, consider how these strengths can address any areas of self-doubt or perceived weaknesses. This step is about channeling your best qualities as a means for personal growth and positive change.

Personal Identity Map

You can explore and visualize the multiple facets of your identity through the powerful exercise of the Personal Identity Map. Creating your identity chart allows you to reflect on the beautiful aspects that shape who you are and understand how societal labels impact your self-perception. This activity not only aids in self-discovery but also enhances understanding and empathy when used to explore the identities of others, whether they are historical figures, fictional characters, or groups.

How to Create Your Personal Identity Map:

- **Design Your Central Identity Space:** Draw a circle or square in the center of a page. The size should be adequate to accommodate the words or phrases you plan to include. This central space can be dedicated to your name or feature a list of words and phrases that you feel define your core identity.
- **Inside the Identity Space:** Inside this shape, jot down words or phrases that resonate with your personal traits or identities. This should include dimensions such as your passions, roles, heritage, beliefs, and distinctive personality traits. This space is meant to reflect the innermost layers of your identity as you see them.
- **Outside the Identity Space:** Outside the central shape, write down labels or descriptions that others might use to describe you or that you perceive society has attributed to you. These could include stereotypes, assigned roles, societal expectations, or

other external perceptions that impact your identity from the outside.

- **Adapt the Map to Your Needs:** The beauty of the Personal Identity Map is its flexibility. The central identity space can adapt to various uses—whether focusing on personal reflection, understanding a historical figure, or dissecting a character in literature. Adjust the exercise to align with your specific objectives, allowing for a personalized approach to exploring identity.

Sections of the Personal Identity Map:

When creating your Personal Identity Map, consider organizing it into sections that capture various elements of your identity. Each section serves as a lens through which to view the multifaceted aspects of who you are and how you relate to the world. Here are some suggested sections to include in your map, each designed to encourage deep reflection and exploration:

- **Personal Attributes:** Traits or qualities you believe define you (e.g., creative, analytical, compassionate).
- **Group Affiliations:** Your connections to ethnic, national, religious, or social groups.
- **Roles and Relationships:** How you see yourself in relation to others (e.g., son, student, friend).
- **Aspirations and Fears:** What drives you forward, and what holds you back?

- **Societal Labels:** You can include positive and negative stereotypes, depending on how society categorizes you.

Using Your Identity Map:

- **Reflect Individually:** Spend time filling out your map thoughtfully. Reflect on each entry and what it means for your sense of identity.
- **Share and Discuss:** Optionally, share your map with classmates, friends, or family. Discussing your identity map can open up conversations about similarities and differences in experiences and perceptions, helping to build understanding and dismantle stereotypes. Please keep the discussion safe and respectful; hearing people and preventing hurtful language or speech is important.
- **Use in Learning Contexts:** In educational settings, use identity maps to deepen discussions about character analysis in literature or the motivations and challenges of historical figures. This helps to humanize complex figures and foster a deeper connection to the material.

Benefits of the Activity:

- **Self-Discovery:** Provides clarity on how you view yourself and how others may view you.
- **Community Building:** Sharing identity maps within a group can help members appreciate diverse backgrounds and build stronger, more respectful connections.

- **Empathy and Understanding:** Helps you and others recognize the complexity of individual identities, reducing prejudice and promoting inclusiveness.

This Personal Identity Map activity is a dynamic tool for growth and understanding, adaptable to many contexts, and beneficial for individuals of all ages. Whether used in educational settings or for personal reflection, it offers valuable insights into our identities' many layers.

Final Thoughts

Consider this chapter a toolkit for constructing a solid foundation for yourself. Throughout, we have delved into the significance of your roots, encountered inspiring heroes whose stories ignite your ambition, begun to create affirmations that resonate with your individual spirit, and engaged in reflective exercises to help you uncover your own strengths and values. This work may be challenging, but it is undeniably the most crucial work you will ever undertake.

Knowing who you are, deep down, is the key to living authentically. It gives you the strength to stand tall, celebrate your differences, and let your true potential shine through.

Remember, personal growth is a continuous process. Don't just read the words in this chapter—embody them. Keep revisiting the exercises, refining, and speaking your affirmations. This is how you cultivate a mindset that's truly your own.

Knowing your worth is just the beginning. Now that you have a strong sense of identity, we'll tackle the next big hurdle: navigating stereotypes, biases, and anyone who tries to limit you. You'll learn how to set healthy boundaries, shut down negativity, and protect your inner peace. It's about turning your identity into a force that helps you overcome any challenge life throws your way.

Get ready to embrace all that you are and all that you can be. True freedom begins with knowing your worth and refusing to let anyone take it away.

RESILIENCE AGAINST STEREOTYPES AND ADVERSITY

As you walk through life, a strong self-image and confidence give you a shine and can often draw extra attention from the people around you. These traits attract admiration, respect, and acknowledgment, showcasing your strength and character. However, they can also bring negative responses, like jealousy, envy, and adversity. For people of color, navigating societal interactions can sometimes mean facing stereotypes. While not always intentional, these assumptions about your character can have profound effects on your confidence and mental state. Recognizing and addressing them calmly and collectively will become a powerful and essential tool in your journey forward.

NAVIGATING STEREOTYPES: STRATEGIES FOR TEENS TO MAINTAIN A POSITIVE SELF-IMAGE

Stereotyping is one of the most frustrating challenges you'll face as a person of color. These harmful assumptions attempt to define you based solely on your race. Stereotypes can sometimes reside in the subconscious, unnoticed by those who carry them—including, perhaps, ourselves at some point in our lives.

Effects of Stereotypes on Self-Identity

Our minds are incredibly absorbent in youth, soaking up influences from our immediate environments—home, daycare, and school. Messages about our "supposed" identities constantly bombard us. Some are awesome and inspiring. Others... not so much. Some of those messages are stereotypes based solely on how you look. These stereotypes try to put you in a box, limiting your potential before you've even had a chance to explore it for yourself. It's important that we, as a society, first and foremost acknowledge that they exist. The next step is to trace these stereotypes back to a source and attempt to understand why they arise.

The Impact of Stereotypes on Identity Development

Stereotypes can distort self-image and self-esteem. When bombarded with negative clichés—like being less intelligent or more likely to be troublesome—based purely on race, it can be challenging to view oneself in a positive light. These stereotypes are not just hurtful but also limiting, placing a box around what you can achieve and who you can become. They can make you question your worth before even giving yourself a chance to prove your capabilities.

Stereotypes in Education

In school settings, these preconceived notions can skew expectations from teachers and peers. For instance, teachers and peers might automatically enroll a Black teen in lower-level classes or discourage them from pursuing challenging academic paths due to biased perceptions of capability. This educational stereotyping affects not only immediate learning opportunities, but can also influence future educational and career aspirations.

Common Stereotypes and Their Transmission

From assuming that Black boys are naturally better at sports than academics to expecting less polite behavior, stereotypes can come from anywhere—even from those with good intentions. Teachers, peers, media representations, and sometimes even family members can transmit these stereotypes, either explicitly through comments or implicitly through behavior and expectations.

Effects on Childhood Development

If left unchallenged, these stereotypes can profoundly affect a young person's development. They can have an impact on everything, from academic performance and social interactions to long-term career choices and personal relationships. A young Black boy might start to limit himself to what he believes is expected of him, not what he aspires to be. Alternatively, he might experience pressure to fit into a specific group due to racial or gender stereotypes, leading to a loss of broader experiences and relationships.

Tips for Countering Stereotypes

Here are a few actionable tips for Black teen boys to help counter these stereotypes:

- **Question and Analyze:** Learn to recognize stereotypes and question their validity. Reflect on where these ideas come from and whether they truly apply to you or your ambitions.
- **Seek Diverse Role Models:** Look for role models in various fields and positions. Seeing successful individuals who look like you can inspire you to break molds and chart your own path.
- **Educate Your Circle:** When safe and appropriate, engage in conversations with friends, family, and educators about the impact of stereotypes. Educating others can help break down the barriers built by misconceptions.
- **Affirm Your Worth:** Use affirmations to build a positive self-image. Regular reminders of your capabilities, worth, and potential can fortify your self-esteem against negative stereotypes.

Not every occurrence warrants a direct challenge to a stereotype. The most effective strategy is to engage thoughtfully, responding to stereotypes in moments when your intervention is likely to be impactful and when you genuinely believe that your perspective can foster understanding or change. This selective approach allows you to use your energy where it's most likely to bring about positive shifts, promote awareness, and foster a more inclusive environment. It's essential to understand how stereotypes can work on two levels:

- **Intentional vs. Unintentional Bias:** Sadly, some people use stereotypes out of malice. However, some people hold these beliefs without even being aware of them, like a bad habit they don't know they have.
- **Choosing Your Battles:** Not every stereotype is worth fighting. Sometimes, the best action is to keep shining and prove them wrong with your actions. But there are moments when calling out ignorance is the right way to create change.

A lack of awareness is common among individuals from vastly different cultures who are only beginning to interact with your community. Immersed in a culture different from your own, you may unknowingly harbor misconceptions. The critical thing to remember is that stereotypes are not the truth about you or anyone else. They can, however, impact how some people see you and, if left unchecked, possibly affect your own self-confidence and image. This makes addressing stereotypes and building your inner strength even more important.

The Broader Impact on Gender Equality

While discussing stereotypes, it's crucial to understand their impact on broader societal issues like gender equality. Gender stereotypes not only limit individual expression but also reinforce harmful societal norms about what men and women can or should do. By challenging these ideas, you free yourself from these constraints and contribute to a more equitable society for everyone.

Let's consider a few stereotypes: the belief that a Black teen boy is destined only for certain types of success, like athletics or entertainment. The reality? Black men excel in all fields, from science and law to art and politics. Understanding this and recognizing the potential within each unique individual is crucial for breaking the cycle of stereotypes.

By confronting and dismantling these stereotypes, you empower yourself and future generations. Overcoming stereotypes is challenging but ultimately rewarding, leading to a more fulfilling and unrestricted expression of who you truly are. Let's continue to break these barriers together, building a foundation for a brighter, more inclusive future.

AFFIRMATIONS AND STORIES OF RESILIENCE TO INSPIRE AND BUILD MENTAL TOUGHNESS

While your affirmations and self-identity are deeply personal, nestled within your own thoughts and perceptions, the challenges they help you confront and the truths they uncover are part of a collective narrative. The Black experience is woven from threads of joy and pain, barriers and breakthroughs. Many of the obstacles you face today are echoes of those encountered by generations before you. This connection underscores the importance of engaging with history—not just as a repository of facts but as a beacon that guides you through current struggles.

As we prepare to craft affirmations that directly challenge stereotypes, it's essential and empowering to draw inspiration from historical and contemporary Black figures who have exemplified resilience and strength in the face of adversity. These individuals endured; some thrived, but all forged paths for others by standing tall against the stereotypes imposed upon them. Their stories are not just history but a source of hope and motivation for us today.

Harriet Tubman

Harriet Tubman became a legendary figure in the fight against slavery. After escaping from bondage in 1849, Tubman didn't just secure her freedom; she made dangerous trips back to the South over the next decade, guiding over 70 enslaved people to freedom via the Underground Railroad. Her courage didn't stop there—during the Civil War, she served in multiple positions in the fight against slavery, such as a scout, spy, and nurse for the Union Army. Tubman's legacy extends far beyond her actions; she symbolizes the fight for freedom and justice, challenging the deeply ingrained stereotypes of Black inferiority and subservience with every step she takes.

Rosa Parks

On December 1, 1955, in Montgomery, Alabama, Rosa Parks made history by refusing to give up her seat to a white man on a bus, sparking the Montgomery Bus Boycott. Her act of defiance became one of the most well-known and iconic moments of the Civil Rights Movement. Rosa Parks was not simply a quiet seamstress; she was a committed activist involved with the NAACP long before her famous stand. The Supreme Court ruled that public bus segregation was unconstitutional following her arrest and the subsequent boycott. Parks' life continued to be one of activism, proving that quiet strength and steadfast resolve can challenge and change systemic injustices.

The Central Park Five

In New York City's Central Park, a white female jogger was raped, and in 1989, five teenagers who were Black and Hispanic were falsely accused and found guilty of the crime. They became known collectively as the Central Park Five. Their convictions were based on coerced confessions, racial bias, and public hysteria rather than physical evidence. The media and public quickly stereotyped these young men as violent criminals, illustrating the dangerous power of racial profiling. In 2002, the real perpetrator's confession and DNA evidence confirmed his guilt, overturning their convictions. The Central Park Five's ordeal is a harrowing reminder of the devastating effects of racial stereotypes and the importance of fighting for justice.

Rubin "Hurricane" Carter

In 1966, middleweight boxer Rubin Carter, also known as "The Hurricane," faced an erroneous conviction for a triple homicide. The wrong conviction ended his promising boxing career due to racial prejudice rather than concrete evidence. Carter's case became a symbol of racial injustice in America, garnering international attention and advocacy from celebrities like Bob Dylan, who wrote a song about his plight. Nearly two decades of appeals and public campaigns finally overturned his conviction in 1985. Carter's story is a testament to the resilience required to fight against deep-seated prejudices and wrongful convictions.

Each of these figures demonstrates the strength to challenge and overcome stereotypes and injustices in their unique contexts. Their stories are not just tales of past struggles but are ongoing reminders of the need for vigilance and advocacy against racial prejudice in today's society. They inspire affirmations of strength, courage, and justice that are particularly meaningful for Blacks navigating similar challenges today.

Identifying Your Heroes

As you craft your affirmations, it's crucial to draw inspiration from heroes whose values and actions resonate with your own principles and aspirations. While all the figures mentioned are great examples, take time to explore the lives of historic Black figures who embody the truths you hold dear. Choose heroes who speak directly to your cause and spirit, just as you personalize your affirmations.

Historical Inspirations

Consider legendary figures like Frederick Douglass and Harriet Tubman, whose courage and eloquence galvanized movements toward freedom and justice. Their lives demonstrate that resilience extends beyond personal endurance—it's about elevating those around you and advocating for collective liberation.

Contemporary Motivations

In more recent history, leaders like Barack Obama and cultural icons such as Maya Angelou have carried forward this legacy. They used their significant platforms to challenge entrenched misconceptions and ignite hope across generations. Their triumphs against systemic obstacles showcase the vast potential each individual has to drive meaningful change.

Drawing Insight and Motivation

From these impactful stories, we gain invaluable insights into perseverance, self-identity, and the transformative power of voice. These narratives do more than motivate— they contextualize our personal battles within a broader historical framework. These individuals did not merely overcome their hurdles; they redefined the pathways for those who would follow, underscoring the profound effects of directly confronting and dismantling stereotypes.

As we proceed to construct our affirmations, let's hold these icons in our thoughts. Their journeys remind us that our struggles are interconnected threads of a larger historical tapestry. Our reactions and actions today can fortify a legacy of strength and resilience. Inspired by their bravery, let us create affirmations that safeguard our self-esteem and boldly affirm our rightful place in the world, unbound by the shackles of stereotypes.

AFFIRMATIONS THAT COUNTER STEREOTYPES AND REINFORCE INNER STRENGTH

To build your armor and counter stereotypes, start by recognizing and acknowledging the stereotypes that affect you personally. Your gender, race, religion, sexual orientation, or any other aspect of your identity can be the basis for stereotypes. Once you've identified these stereotypes, remind yourself that they are false generalizations, often rooted in ignorance and prejudice. Immerse yourself in a community of supportive and empowering individuals who support your aspirations and see greatness within you. Educate yourself about the diversity of experiences within your own identity group, and challenge stereotypes with knowledge and understanding. Remember, just as heroes and icons confront their foes with courage, you can conquer stereotypes and rise above the limitations they try to impose on you.

Common Stereotypes Faced by Young Black Men

Let's break down some typical stereotypes you might face and arm you with affirmations to obliterate them:

Stereotype: Black men are not as intelligent as other races.

- **Situation:** This might crop up in educational settings, where you could encounter this bias from peers or even teachers.
- **Affirmation:** "My intelligence knows no bounds. I am a dedicated and capable learner, achieving high marks through my perseverance and intellect."

Stereotype: Black men are athletic but not suited for scholarly success.

- **Situation:** This stereotype might pressure you to focus solely on sports, overshadowing your academic aspirations.
- **Affirmation:** "I excel in both academics and athletics. I am multifaceted, with a mind as strong as my body."

Stereotype: Black men are aggressive or dangerous.

- **Situation:** This damaging stereotype can follow you in various interactions, whether you're walking down the street or encountering law enforcement.
- **Affirmation:** "I am composed and dignified. I approach every interaction with respect and self-control, ensuring my presence is reassuring, not threatening."

Crafting Your Own Affirmations

These examples are just starting points. Reflect on personal examples of how stereotypes have impacted you. Create affirmations that speak to those experiences, using the strength shown by your role models as inspiration.

Implementing Your Affirmations

In School: When underestimated, let your affirmations remind you of your capability and previous successes.

In Social Settings: Use affirmations to maintain your integrity when stereotypes try to label your actions.

Online: Counter negative stereotypes on social platforms by reaffirming your true identity and values.

Personalizing Your Affirmations

While the examples provided are foundational, true power comes from personal relevance. Adapt these affirmations to align with your journey, challenges, and the virtues you aspire to embody. Draw inspiration from how your heroes represented themselves and their visions for the future.

Moving Forward

Remember, affirmations gain their strength from belief and repetition. They are not mere phrases but declarations of your truth, fortifying your self-image against the erosive effects of stereotypes. Each time you recite an affirmation, you're not just countering negativity but reinforcing a positive, resilient self-identity that resonates with your highest aspirations.

By embracing this practice, you rewrite the narrative surrounding your identity, transforming stereotypes into opportunities for empowerment and affirmation. Let's build on this solid foundation, creating affirmations celebrating our value and potential.

ACTIVITIES TO TRANSFORM CHALLENGES INTO STEPPING STONES FOR GROWTH

Building personal affirmations is a powerful tool for cultivating a stronger, more resilient self-identity. To empower you on this journey, we've curated a list of activities designed to transform your challenges into stepping stones toward personal growth. Consider these activities as your allies, reinforcing the positive mindset that your affirmations instill and giving you control over your self-identity.

Activities to Complement Your Affirmations

1. Journaling:

- **Purpose:** Deepen your self-awareness and track your progress.
- **Activity:** Regularly write about your experiences with stereotypes or challenges and how you've used your affirmations to handle them. Reflect on how your thoughts and feelings change over time.
- **Benefit:** It provides a tangible record of your growth and helps clarify your thoughts.

2. Role-Playing:

- **Purpose:** Role-playing allows you to practice responding to situations where you encounter stereotypes, preparing you for real-life interactions.

- **Activity:** With a friend or mentor, role-play scenarios where you might face stereotypes. Use your affirmations to assertively respond in these simulations.
- **Benefit:** Builds confidence and prepares you for real-life interactions.

3. Reading and Research:

- **Purpose:** Gain inspiration and learn from the experiences of others.
- **Activity:** Read books or watch documentaries about individuals who have overcome adversity. Study how they handled situations similar to yours.
- **Benefit:** Provides a broader perspective and additional strategies for resilience.

4. Peer Discussion Groups:

- **Purpose:** Share experiences and strategies with others.
- **Activity:** Join or form a discussion group where members can openly talk about personal challenges related to stereotypes and share affirmation techniques. This fosters a sense of community, where you can feel supported and understood in your journey.
- **Benefit:** Encourages mutual support and offers diverse approaches to similar issues.

5. Creative Expression:

- **Purpose:** Channel emotions and reinforce your affirmations through art.
- **Activity:** Use arts like drawing, music, or writing poetry to express how you feel about the stereotypes you encounter and visualize your triumphs.
- **Benefit:** Helps process emotions creatively and solidifies your personal narrative.

Integrating Activities With Affirmations

Integration: To make the most of these activities, integrate them closely with the affirmations you've developed. This way, you can continuously reinforce and expand your affirmations based on your learnings and experiences.

Keep in mind that these exercises aim to do more than reinforce your affirmations. They also aim to integrate them into your daily routine, transforming them into useful resources as you work towards strengthening your self-identity. As you engage in these activities, you'll discover that each challenge you overcome not only builds your resilience but also adds a rung to your ladder of personal growth, instilling a sense of hope and motivation.

Gratitude and Growth Reflections

Welcome to the Gratitude and Growth Reflections section of your personal development journey. This exercise encourages daily reflection to boost self-awareness and foster gratitude. Each day offers new experiences and interactions, which can be rich sources of personal growth and lessons learned.

This activity encourages you to document notable events, breakthroughs, or everyday interactions from your week. Reflecting on these moments can reveal patterns in your behavior, highlight areas for improvement, and underscore what you are truly grateful for in life.

Directions: For each day of the week, list significant occurrences, insights gained, and expressions of gratitude. This structured reflection helps you identify how daily experiences shape your character and influence your overall well-being.

Example:

- **Thursday**: Had dinner with Jay and Molly. Finished the work on the deck.
- **Lessons Learned**: Realized the importance of generosity and discovered that challenges often seem more daunting before they are confronted.
- **Grateful for**: The opportunity to learn from friends and the resources to improve my living space.

Use this worksheet as a tool to deepen your understanding of yourself and to foster a mindset that values growth and gratitude. By the end of the week, review your entries to identify any emerging patterns and plan how to approach the next week with even more positivity and purpose.

Gratitude and Growth Reflections

Sunday:

Lessons Learned:

Grateful for:

Monday:

Lessons Learned:

Grateful for:

Tuesday:

Lessons Learned:

Grateful for:

Wednesday:

Lessons Learned:

Grateful for:

Midweek Reflection:

Any patterns so far this week?

Ways to Finish Out The Week on a Higher Note:

Thursday:

Lessons Learned:

Grateful for:

Friday:

Lessons Learned:

Grateful for:

Saturday:
Lessons Learned:
Grateful for:
End of Week Reflection:
Any patterns throughout the week:
Best three lessons learned and why:
1.
2.
3.
Thoughts for Improvement Next Week:
Weekly Challenge:
Complete a goal:
Help a friend:
Try Something New:

Final Thoughts

In this chapter, we've delved into the transformative power of affirmations and the importance of resilience in the face of stereotypes and adversity. Understanding and implementing the discussed practices equips you to fortify your self-image against arising challenges, using them as stepping stones rather than stumbling blocks.

We've seen how affirmations can reshape our perception of ourselves, helping us to stand tall and confident despite external pressures. It's important to take these lessons to heart and actively incorporate them into your daily life. Each affirmation you craft and recite reinforces your strength and your right to aspire to greatness.

As you move forward, I encourage you to put these powerful tools into practice. Begin each day with affirmations that remind you of your worth and capabilities, and watch as your reality transforms to match your beliefs.

The upcoming chapter will build on the foundation of resilience by delving into topics such as embracing leadership roles, building confidence, and making a positive impact on your community. You've learned how to protect and uplift yourself; now, let's explore how you can extend that strength outward and foster change. This next part of your journey will help you transform your teen years into a period of significant growth and lasting impact, laying down a foundation of unshakeable strength and positive habits. Join me as we discover how stepping into your power can open new paths and opportunities.

CONFIDENCE, LEADERSHIP, AND COMMUNITY

> "The ultimate measure of a man is not where he stands in moments of comfort and convenience, but where he stands at times of challenge and controversy."
>
> — MARTIN LUTHER KING JR.

In the face of adversity, true leaders emerge—not just by their ability to rise individually but by their capacity to uplift others along the way. Leadership is a profound expression of character, visible both to oneself and to the world. Leaders not only forge paths to success but also extend a hand to guide those behind them.

In this chapter, we explore how affirmations can be a powerful tool to cultivate and sustain a leadership mindset. You will learn about the essential qualities that define a leader, understand the pivotal roles leaders play in our communities, and discover how to confidently embody a leader's mindset.

Let's embark on this journey to harness your potential and embrace leadership responsibilities.

COMMUNITY LEADERS' CRUCIAL ROLE: GUIDANCE AND REPRESENTATION

Community leaders play a crucial role in shaping not only the internal dynamics of their communities but also their global perception. Leadership entails navigating your community through challenges and representing it amidst ever-developing societal norms and expectations. As we advocate for the acceptance of new communities and fight for their rightful place on the global stage, we continually redefine societal norms and expectations, determining what is socially acceptable or unacceptable, fair or unfair, right or wrong.

The Black community, in particular, is still engaged in many of these battles. As a potential leader, acknowledging the existence of these struggles is a crucial first step, much like we seek acknowledgment of the struggles of our own community. How a leader represents their community—balancing both guidance and representation—will significantly determine their effectiveness. A leader's ability to navigate these dual roles adeptly is vital for steering the community through the complexities of modern societal changes while ensuring that the international community hears and respects its voice.

Guidance Through Knowledge and Empathy

People seek leaders for guidance because leaders exemplify resilience and possess a deep understanding of their community's needs. Their direct experiences with the community's challenges uniquely qualify them to craft effective strategies and solutions. These leaders are more than just planners and initiators; they are beacons of hope and symbols of strength, showcasing profound empathy, fortitude, and an unwavering commitment to justice and equality. They inspire trust and provide direction, helping their communities navigate times of uncertainty and change.

Leadership can take on various forms. It is important to remember that being an effective leader does not mean you have to follow a high-profile path, such as becoming a U.S. President. While Barack Obama's journey is inspirational, he represents an extraordinary example of leadership, benefiting from a unique combination of hard work and rare opportunities that might not be available to everyone. Effective leadership doesn't require such exceptional paths; it's about maximizing your unique talents and seizing the opportunities that are accessible to you.

Each person's path to leadership will differ. Your effectiveness as a leader comes from how well you can leverage your distinct talents and opportunities, not from mirroring someone else's journey. The most critical step in your leadership journey is to chart your own path, crafting a style that reflects your personal strengths and the specific needs of your community. Embrace your unique perspective and capabilities, and use them to foster change and growth within your community.

Representation: Carrying the Community's Voice

Individuals assume immense responsibility as leaders, serving as the community's representatives and embodying their identity and values on a global stage. People often perceive a leader's actions, speech, demeanor, and even appearance as direct reflections of the community's character and ethos. The fairness of having a community's diverse and unique identity represented by a single person may be debatable. Still, this form of representation is a reality that carries significant weight.

Recognizing that there is a prevalent expectation—both within and outside the community—for leaders to effectively embody the collective spirit and aspirations, despite the challenges, is crucial. Like parents expect their children to uphold family values and present themselves respectfully, community members expect similar conduct from their leaders.

The concept of representation goes beyond mere appearance or conduct; it involves a deep embodiment of the community's history, its struggles, and its achievements. Leaders need to be aware that their actions and decisions not only shape their own perception but also how outsiders perceive and treat the entire community.

A good leader understands the importance of representation and strives to showcase the community in the best possible light. This doesn't mean conforming to the acceptance principles of other communities but being mindful and deliberate in their public and internal community interactions. They maintain a keen awareness that, as a symbol, their actions and words have the power to significantly influence and shape the community's image on a larger scale.

Black Teen Boys' Role in Setting Positive Examples Within Their Communities:

The Black community urgently requires leaders who fully understand the unique challenges Black individuals face today. Black youth are especially poised to grasp these issues. Each generation encounters obstacles that, while similar, demand specific solutions that adapt to the rapidly evolving global landscape. The insights from Black youth are particularly critical, offering fresh perspectives that reflect the diverse facets of the Black experience.

Contemporary systems of education, justice, and their effectiveness, along with interactions with external communities, are all areas where young Black men and women navigate complex dynamics. These interactions often determine how different groups perceive the Black community, making the viewpoints of young Black individuals invaluable. As global society grows and becomes more interconnected, Black youth frequently find themselves at the forefront of these cross-cultural exchanges.

Given the diverse environments in which Black youth interact, they are, in many ways, already functioning as leaders. For many, their first exposure to Black culture comes through interactions with young Black individuals. This places young Black men and women in a pivotal position, significantly shaping how others—and potentially future generations—perceive the Black community.

Therefore, it is crucial for young Black individuals to arm themselves with the appropriate mindset, tools, and perceptions to manage these interactions effectively. They must articulate their stances, opinions, and community image with clarity and confidence. Affirmations are a potent tool in this regard, boosting confidence during new interactions and reinforcing a leadership mindset.

These interactions not only influence external perceptions but also inspire and guide the Black community from within. In many ways, young Black individuals have always acted as ambassadors for their communities. While this responsibility may be daunting and not of their choosing, it is nevertheless present. By accepting this role, young Black leaders can set a precedent for their community and others, becoming pillars of support and catalysts for the change that is desperately needed.

This influential position isn't just about traditional leadership; it involves embodying leadership qualities in daily interactions. By doing so, young Black leaders can forge pathways for positive change and deeper understanding within the Black community and broader society. This is a call to young Black individuals to rise as leaders, using their unique positions to effect meaningful change and to challenge and redefine perceptions through their actions and words.

A Newer Tomorrow: Young Black Leaders

As we explore the impact young Black individuals are having in their communities and beyond, let's meet some dynamic young leaders who have embraced the challenge of making a difference:

David Onilude

In Nigeria, David Onilude recognized the transformative power of technology and launched a project to foster digital and media literacy. His initiative quickly evolved into Tech Now Global, a nonprofit established in 2020 that combats digital illiteracy by equipping rural youth with the necessary skills and resources. David, through Tech Now Global, is committed to equipping his generation and future generations with essential 21st-century skills to thrive in the digital age (Channel Kindness, 2023).

Amanda Gorman

At just 23 years old, Amanda Gorman captured the nation's heart with her inauguration poem, "The Hill We Climb," which eloquently echoed themes of unity and resilience. Her performance at the 2021 Presidential Inauguration, following the tumultuous 2020 U.S. Election and the Capitol storming, drew acclaim from figures like Lin-Manuel Miranda and Barack Obama. A Harvard alum and the first-ever National Youth Poet Laureate, Gorman's work frequently explores issues of feminism, racial injustice, and the African Diaspora. In 2021, she co-hosted the Met Gala, highlighting her influence in literary and cultural spheres (Biron, 2022).

Jerome Foster II

Jerome Foster II is a climate justice advocate who founded OneMillionOfUs. This organization mobilized a million young voters for the 2020 U.S. Election. His commitment to environmental issues extends through his recent co-founding of an organization that comprehensively uses creative storytelling to address the climate crisis. Jerome's work emphasizes the urgency of sustainable practices and active political participation among youth (Channel Kindness, 2023).

Autumn Grant

Captivated by politics since third grade, Autumn is a fierce advocate for empowering young Black women within the political sphere. She founded the first Black Girls Vote chapter at American University, focusing on Black women's unique challenges in political engagement. Her work addresses critical issues like childcare needs, socioeconomic factors, and voter suppression in urban and minority communities. Now serving as Chief of Staff for Maryland State Senator Arthur Ellis, Autumn continues to drive change and encourage political involvement among Black women at multiple levels.

These young leaders are challenging existing barriers and setting new benchmarks for leadership. Their stories inspire others to take action and affirm that leadership can manifest in many impactful ways.

The Need for Role Models Within Our Communities

Our communities are filled with young individuals seeking sources of guidance and inspiration as they navigate the many paths of life. Some will need more help than others; our lives vary in challenges as our families do in the support they can offer, and community role models can make all the difference here. Even the most troubled youth can find hope in a role model who demonstrates a willingness to support and suggests potential paths to pursue. Role models are mentors and so much more; they are symbols of hope and guides to new possibilities.

The role models within our communities are not just individuals who have achieved success or a sense of accomplishment. They are living, breathing inspirations; their stories and presence within the community instill a sense of hope and aspiration in the hearts and minds of the young. People revere them for their journeys and cherish their contributions to the community, whether they are in the form of hope or support. They are the voice and embodiment of the communities they hail from, a testament to our collective spirit's strength and resilience.

Role models appear in various forms within our communities, ranging from direct community involvement to leadership roles in churches, schools, and mentorship programs or through distinguished public and professional endeavors that earn the respect of their community.

The presence of respected and relatable role models plays a critical role in the development of black teen boys, helping them find their own paths to leadership and responsibility within their communities. As Breland-Noble observed, seeing individuals who resemble them and are admired in roles of influence, such as leading church services or performing in significant events, significantly contributes to their self-esteem and aspirations. "It helps children of color to see people they look up to, who also look like them," notes DeAngelis (2014), highlighting the powerful impact of such role models.

It's crucial to recognize the positive effects of representation—seeing a role model who looks like them or comes from a similar background can profoundly inspire young people. This visibility fosters confidence and helps youth develop a more positive outlook on life. It empowers them to be themselves boldly and authentically, providing a solid foundation upon which they can build their futures.

Moreover, role models shape not only the perspectives of the youth who admire them but also influence the broader community's view. They set standards and exemplify the values and virtues that others aspire to emulate. Their actions and success stories reverberate, setting a benchmark for achievement and ethical conduct within the community. This ripple effect of inspiration and leadership enhances the community's overall vitality and cohesiveness, proving that the impact of role models extends far beyond individual interactions.

AFFIRMATIONS TO FOSTER SELF-CONFIDENCE AND LEADERSHIP SKILLS

As emerging leaders, one of the foundational qualities we must cultivate is self-confidence. Renowned leaders are often recognized for their pronounced confidence, enabling them to overcome challenges, face adversity head-on, and recover from setbacks gracefully. Developing self-confidence doesn't require external resources like a gym or a trainer; it's an inner strength you can build on your own, with your conscience as your ally. Let's explore how to craft affirmations that bolster confidence and assertiveness, preparing you for effective leadership.

Defining Self-Confidence

Self-confidence is more than feeling good about yourself; it's a deep-seated belief in your ability to manage life's challenges, interact productively with others, and confidently communicate your ideas. It is the trust you place in yourself to make decisions, take action, and advocate for yourself and others.

The Importance of Self-Confidence

- **Resilience and Adaptability:** Confident leaders can quickly bounce back from setbacks. Instead of seeing insurmountable obstacles, they view challenges as opportunities to develop and improve themselves.

- **Assertiveness and Effective Communication:** A self-assured leader communicates their thoughts and needs clearly and respectfully without infringing on the rights of others. This skill is crucial in negotiations, problem-solving, and healthy interpersonal relationships.
- **Goal Achievement:** Self-confidence empowers you to set realistic goals and persistently pursue them. It provides the stamina to continue striving toward your objectives, even when progress seems slow.
- **Reduced Anxiety and Stress:** When you believe in your capabilities, you're less likely to feel overwhelmed by pressure or stress. Confidence promotes a more positive and proactive approach to life's stresses.
- **Increased Self-Worth and Self-Esteem:** Building self-confidence significantly influences how you value and perceive yourself. It enhances your sense of self-worth and overall life satisfaction.

Crafting Affirmations for Confidence and Assertiveness

Here are some affirmations you can start with to foster these traits. Feel free to tailor these affirmations to better suit your specific context, as the ones that resonate with you personally will be the most effective.

1. I trust my ability and see my potential to lead.
2. I stand firm in the face of challenges. Courage and confidence come from learning from every experience and from embracing my failures rather than fearing them.

3. I communicate my ideas clearly and assertively, and I show respect for myself and others.
4. I am resilient, adaptable, and ever-learning as I navigate the challenges and circumstances life presents me.
5. Every step, big or small, builds strength and reaffirms my self-assurance.

IDEAS AND INITIATIVES FOR COMMUNITY ENGAGEMENT: DEVELOPING LEADERSHIP THROUGH SERVICE

Embarking on your community journey is the first stride toward leadership, and it's simpler than you might imagine. Your community likely has message boards with postings for events and volunteer work at churches and community centers. The internet is a treasure trove of community leaders you can reach out to and explore potential volunteer opportunities. If you have a unique approach, don't hesitate to share it with them. Let's delve into some of the more common and practical ways to get engaged in your local community.

Exploring Your Interests in Community Settings: Communities are rich sources of opportunities waiting to be tapped. Whether you have musical talents to share at local events, an interest in teaching or learning new skills, or a passion for sports, there's likely a venue in your community where you can contribute:

1. **Workshops and Skills Sharing:** Look for local workshops that align with your interests. Many community centers offer classes where you can both learn and teach. From language exchanges to cooking classes at local shelters, every skill you share or learn can have a positive ripple effect.
2. **Sports and Recreation:** Participate in local sports leagues or consider managing sports events. These activities promote health and wellness and teach important leadership skills, such as teamwork, strategic planning, and public speaking.

Direct Community Engagement Ideas

1. **Animal Care:** Pets are a beloved part of many communities. While volunteering at animal shelters or organizing pet supply drives are excellent ways to help, consider starting smaller by walking or pet-sitting for neighbors. This not only enables you to connect with community members but also gives you insight into the responsibilities of pet care.
2. **Senior Support:** Visiting elder care facilities or assisting elderly neighbors with everyday tasks can make a significant difference in their lives. Whether helping with grocery shopping, technology, or just chatting, your support can significantly enhance their quality of life.
3. **Youth Mentorship:** Becoming a mentor through programs like Big Brothers Big Sisters can profoundly impact young lives. Offer guidance as a tutor, participate in after-school programs, or help organize youth-focused activities. Your knowledge

and attention can help foster a safer and more supportive environment for the next generation.

4. **Support for Those Less Fortunate:** Issues involving people experiencing homelessness and those disadvantaged in life are always present. Even small acts to help remedy these problems can have a significant impact. Volunteering at shelters, donating to local organizations and nonprofits, or participating in food drives are great ways to get involved. You could also advocate for policy changes that address the causes of homelessness.

5. **Community Work:** Community Gardens, Churches, Food Banks, and Local Environmental Clean-up projects are great ways to help your community. You'll improve its conditions and meet others who share your interests and pursuits; establishing healthy community relationships is an essential part of leadership.

Supporting Your Family

Remember, charity begins at home. Prioritize meeting your family's needs before expanding your efforts. Simple acts like offering childcare, helping with homework, or assisting family members with transport can strengthen your familial ties and set a strong foundation for your external community work.

Fundraising and Awareness Campaigns

When you're ready to take your community involvement to the next level, consider leading or participating in fundraising campaigns. You could direct these efforts towards local enhancements like purchasing new books for the library, or towards more significant causes like promoting human rights awareness. Organizing sales, auctions, or community events raises funds and brings people together for a common purpose.

As you step out to make a difference, remember that your efforts can substantially transform your community. Each initiative you undertake builds a network of support and trust that benefits others and enriches your leadership skills and personal growth.

Brainstorm Sheet

Below is a brainstorm sheet for jotting down project ideas and setting goals. You can trace out each of the steps needed to finish your project or achieve your goal. Take time to reflect on your projects and the work they can do for your community.

Brainstorm Worksheet

Project Ideas:

What are you interested in? How can you use it for the community?

What can you do to support your community?

Goal Setting:

What do you hope to accomplish?

How break your main goal down into smaller achievable goals?

Planning:

What resources or help do you need?

How long do you have to start?

Anything you need but can't get?

Make a list of steps to complete your goal. Add a timeline if you have one:

1.

2.

3.

4.

5.

6.

Impact:

List the positive ways this will impact your community:

1.

2.

3.

Reflect:

How did your plan workout?

What went right/wrong?

What can you do to improve on the next try?

Final Thoughts

As we conclude this chapter, remember that developing leadership skills and building confidence are foundational steps toward making a positive impact in your community and beyond. We've explored how to cultivate these qualities and apply them effectively; now it's your turn to put these ideas into action. Step forward with the affirmations and strategies you've learned, and start making a difference today.

With newfound confidence and a blueprint for leadership, you're well on your way to carving out a path of meaningful success. In the next chapter, we'll delve into how to channel this leadership and confidence into achieving your academic and career goals. We have the ability to transform your aspirations into achievable goals, providing you with the necessary resources to confront difficulties and take advantage of opportunities that lie ahead. Get ready to set clear objectives, harness your strengths, and move steadily toward the future you envision.

The Power of Your Thoughts; The Power of Your Words

"You cannot win the war against the world if you can't win the war against your own mind."

— WILL SMITH

You might remember from the introduction how good an example of shaping your own destiny Will Smith is, and it's him I'd like you to keep in mind as you continue on your journey. He was a young Black man just like you, facing the same struggles; he decided what he wanted for his future and he took it. It's easy to think that the kind of success Smith saw isn't possible for us, but he's a shining example of the fact that it is.

It's true that as Black men we face particular challenges, but that means that understanding the power of our thoughts is even more important. As Smith said, we must win the war against our own minds if we're going to have any chance of winning the war against the world. Our thoughts are powerful, and they become our reality. What you're learning in this book is how to shape those thoughts to create the reality you want to live, and that's something that's so important for young Black people. I want as many people as possible to realize this and take their destinies into their own hands, and now you're so far along on this journey, your understanding of your own power forever changed, I'd like to ask you to help me reach them.

By leaving a review of this book on Amazon, you'll help this book get into the hands of more of the young Black men who need it.

Your thoughts have more power than you might have realized, and so do your words. By leaving your thoughts on this book online, you'll help others see that this is possible for them too, and inspire them to take the steps they need to shape their own future.

Our destiny is in our own hands, but the support of others is crucial too, and when we stick together and help each other out, we become a powerful force. As Black men, we face judgment every day, and that can wear us down: Let's change the narrative, and together, become the change we want to see in the world.

Scan the QR code below

ENVISIONING SUCCESS—
ACADEMICS AND CAREER

Our modern society frequently gauges success by academic achievements and career milestones. Working hard or taking advantage of opportunities to accomplish these goals is not enough. It is essential to possess a mindset that is both positive and resilient. Setting clear milestones and measuring progress incrementally are crucial steps for staying motivated and preventing burnout in these enduring pursuits. Affirmations play a vital role in this process, helping students and professionals fuel their ambitions and realize more rewarding outcomes. This chapter explores practical goal-setting strategies and visualization techniques that can amplify your success path. By integrating affirmations into your daily routine, we aim to strengthen your confidence and assertiveness, enabling you to overcome challenges and stay intensely focused on your goals.

AFFIRMATIONS FOR ACADEMIC MOTIVATION AND ENVISIONING CAREER SUCCESS

Let's explore various scenarios that test the effectiveness of academic affirmations. This will show you how affirmations can work wonders in your life.

Academic Scenario: Taking on a New Language

Title: Expanding Horizons

First-Person Perspective:

The allure of distant places has captivated me since I was young. Each time I look at a map or spin a globe, I feel a strong pull toward the diverse cultures and languages scattered across the world. My goal is ambitious but clear: I want to learn at least three languages, starting with Spanish. However, the thought of beginning this journey fills me with hesitation. I already have a full academic schedule and am struggling to keep up with my current classes.

I reached out to a friend who recently took the Spanish class I'm interested in. His feedback wasn't exactly encouraging. He described the course as "brutal," mentioning a very strict teacher and a workload that's double that of other classes. Despite these challenges, my genuine excitement about learning Spanish fuels my determination. I'm ready to take on this new challenge, even with my busy schedule filled with basketball practices, household chores, and other studies.

Effect on the Belief System:

This dilemma has me questioning my capacity to manage my time and handle additional responsibilities. The fear of overextending myself is real, and it's casting a shadow over my enthusiasm for pursuing a goal I'm passionate about. The prospect of additional stress from a challenging course could impact not just my academic performance but also my overall well-being.

Positive Affirmations:

1. "I can manage my time effectively to pursue my passions."

- This affirmation helps me trust in my ability to organize and prioritize my activities, ensuring I can meet my academic responsibilities while also making room for personal growth.

2. "Every step in learning something new is progress, no matter the pace."

- Reminding myself that learning is a personal journey and that each bit of new knowledge is a victory keeps me motivated to persist, regardless of challenges.

3. "I am resilient and can adapt to new challenges."

- This statement boosts my confidence, reinforcing that I have the strength to adapt to demanding situations and can handle the stress that might come with them.

4. "I make room in my life for what matters to me, and I control my schedule."

- It's empowering to remember that I have the autonomy to make decisions about how I spend my time and what priorities I set.

Reaffirmed Belief System:

These affirmations not only encourage me to reevaluate how I view my capabilities and time management, but they also instill a sense of resilience and adaptability. They bolster my confidence, reminding me that I have control over my choices and that adjusting my commitments to accommodate my interests is possible. By reaffirming these beliefs, I am more prepared to take on the Spanish course, knowing that it aligns with my broader aspirations and that I am equipped to manage the challenges it brings.

Affirmations for Academic Success

Here is a list of affirmations you can use to help guide you to success in school. Remember that while these affirmations are a good start, you should always tailor them to best suit your unique situation.

1. "Every day, my brain's capacity to acquire and retain knowledge is expanding."

- **Situation:** Use this affirmation when preparing for exams or learning new material to enhance retention and understanding.

2. "I have a sharp mind, which makes me an outstanding student."

- **Situation:** Repeat this when you doubt your intellectual abilities, especially before tests or presentations.

3. "I have a winner's mindset and love accomplishing my goals."

- **Situation:** Ideal for setting and pursuing short-term and long-term academic or career objectives.

4. "I am advancing to new levels by learning more each day."

- **Situation:** Helpful during continuous learning phases or when advancing your studies or job skills.

5. "I feel thankful to be a student, and it shows."

- **Situation:** Use when feeling overwhelmed or unenthusiastic about your studies to foster gratitude and positive engagement.

Career Scenario: Work Dilemmas

Title: Overcoming Imposter Syndrome

First-Person Perspective:

Here I am, freshly initiated into an internship at one of the city's most prestigious tech startups—an opportunity I dreamed of and worked hard to secure. Yet, instead of excitement, I find myself gripped by anxiety each night, haunted by the fear that I might be underperforming. Despite receiving mostly positive reviews and performing on par with, if not better than, most of my fellow interns, my confidence is on shaky ground. A few interns are excelling beyond expectations, and here I am, battling a persistent feeling of inadequacy. I know I'm not alone in this struggle, as imposter syndrome is a common experience among many professionals and interns.

As one of the few Black individuals and the only new Black intern, I feel immense pressure to prove myself. I carry the weight of broader expectations, representing not just my capabilities but those of my community. This week has been particularly tough. I need to catch up on a project from yesterday, and a recent talk with my boss about my work last week has only amplified my fears, leaving me tense and doubting my abilities. But I am not alone in this. Our community is strong and resilient, and we have the power to overcome these challenges.

Effect on Belief System:

This situation is testing my self-esteem and professional confidence. The fear of not living up to expectations—both my own and those perceived by others—is challenging my sense of belonging and worthiness at this internship. I am wrestling with the worry that any misstep may reflect poorly not just on myself but also on my community, further feeding into my anxiety and affecting my performance. This constant self-doubt and fear of failure are taking a toll on my mental health, making it difficult for me to fully enjoy my internship and perform at my best.

Positive Affirmations:

1. "I am competent and bring valuable skills to my team."

- This affirmation reminds me to trust in my abilities and the hard work that got me here, reinforcing that I am fully capable of handling the responsibilities of my internship.

2. "I grow and learn from every challenge I face."

- Approaching every obstacle as a chance to develop assists in lessening apprehension and transforms conceivable impediments into teachings that amplify my proficiency and self-assurance.

3. "I deserve my place here and represent my community with integrity and strength."

- This statement bolsters my confidence, emphasizing that my presence in this competitive environment is well-deserved and that I embody the resilience and capability of my community.

4. "Each day, I am improving and proving my worth through my dedication and hard work."

- Regularly affirming my commitment to personal excellence helps me focus on my progress and continuous improvement rather than on any temporary setbacks.

Reaffirmed Belief System:

These affirmations serve as crucial mental reinforcements that help counteract the negative thoughts stemming from imposter syndrome. They enable me to recalibrate my self-perception, reminding me of my achievements and the positive attributes I bring to my role. With these affirmations, I can rebuild my confidence, reduce my anxiety, and enhance my performance, ensuring that I not only meet but exceed the expectations set before me. They remind me that I am here not by chance but through merit, and every day is a new opportunity to showcase my capabilities and contribute meaningfully to my team. Self-affirmations are a powerful tool that can empower us to take control of our self-perception and overcome imposter syndrome.

Affirmations for Career Success

Affirmations are a powerful tool for fostering a positive mindset and overcoming challenges in your professional life. They can enhance your self-confidence, bolster your resolve, and keep you focused on your career goals. Here's a list of affirmations tailored for career success. Remember, personalizing these to fit the unique challenges and aspirations of your career will make them even more effective.

1. **"I am worthy of my career aspirations and capable of achieving them."**

- **Situation:** Use this affirmation to boost your self-esteem and reinforce your belief in your professional capabilities, especially when aiming for promotions or tackling ambitious projects.

2. "I attract success and prosperity with my ideas."

- **Situation:** Ideal for those in creative or strategic roles, this affirmation helps maintain a positive outlook and a mindset conducive to innovation and impactful contributions.

3. "Every challenge offers a valuable lesson to enhance my career."

- **Situation:** This affirmation is useful when facing obstacles or setbacks. It shifts your perspective to view challenges as opportunities for growth and learning.

4. "My contributions are valuable and recognized by my colleagues and superiors."

- **Situation:** Encourage feelings of self-worth and recognition in your work environment, particularly useful for those feeling undervalued or overlooked.

5. "I communicate clearly and effectively to manifest success in my projects."

- **Situation:** Great for professionals who frequently engage in presentations, meetings, or negotiations, this affirmation helps hone communication skills.

Regular use of these affirmations can truly transform your ability to maintain a positive mindset, conquer challenges, and reach your academic and career goals. The secret to their effectiveness lies in the power of positive thinking. By consistently affirming positive statements about your capabilities and aspirations, you can reprogram your mind to genuinely believe in your potential for success. This newfound belief amplifies your confidence and sharpens your determination and focus, empowering you to tackle new challenges and stay resolute in your pursuits.

Additionally, affirmations serve as vital reminders of your objectives, helping to keep your goals clear and centered in your daily actions. Visualization techniques, in tandem with positive affirmations, enable you to form a clear and detailed mental picture of attaining your objectives. This, in turn, provides added inspiration to follow through with the actions required to transform your aspirations into actual accomplishments. By integrating practical goal-setting strategies with affirmations and visualization, you fuel your ambitions and pave the way for profound success in our competitive modern society. Remember, these affirmations are adaptable to your specific circumstances. They are a tool designed to cater to your unique journey, helping to smooth the path to your ultimate success.

SETTING AND ACHIEVING GOALS: STRATEGIES FOR ACADEMIC EXCELLENCE AND CAREER PLANNING

When planning your academic path and career, it is essential to consider what you want to achieve and whether time is a factor. To create a well-researched plan, you must determine your desires, assess the time required to reach your goals, anticipate potential obstacles, and develop strategies to overcome them. Setting milestones for beginners is also crucial to getting started.

SMART Planning

The SMART goal-setting technique is an effective approach to setting goals. This method allows you to clearly visualize and define your goals, understand their purpose, and establish objectives to guide you toward success.

The ASVAB Career Exploration Program defines the acronym SMART as so:

Specific: Outline your goal clearly and in as much detail as possible. Really think about what you want to pursue and the purpose it serves. You'll want to put your needs first, as this will be the path you set forth. Still, be mindful of the voices and concerns of those around you. Despite the differences in their dreams or thoughts about your purpose, listening to them always yields wisdom, concern, and various forms of guidance.

Measurable: It's essential to clearly define how you will measure your success across various areas of your life. Set concrete metrics that resonate with your specific goals. For professionals, this might involve aiming for promotions or reaching specific financial milestones. For students, measurable goals could include:

- Achieving higher grades.
- Increasing the number of books read per month.
- Allocating a fixed number of hours for study each week.

If your focus is on personal development, such as mastering a new skill or hobby, establish clear benchmarks, like learning a designated number of songs on an instrument or completing a project by a certain date.

These measurable standards are crucial for recognizing when you achieve your goals and making necessary adjustments along your journey. It's common to feel overwhelmed and need to scale back, or conversely, to find that you're progressing rapidly and wish to accelerate your efforts. Pre-set, quantifiable objectives allow you to flexibly adjust your goals, either advancing them further in your timeline or extending them to ensure continuous growth and challenge. This adaptability in goal setting helps maintain your momentum and keeps your objectives aligned with your evolving capabilities and circumstances.

Attainable: When setting goals, it's important that they are challenging yet within your reach. Begin with goals that are akin to hills—manageable challenges that build your confidence and skills as you prepare for larger, more ambitious objectives. Your goals should stretch your capabilities but remain achievable; this balance is crucial to avoid overconfidence while still acknowledging and harnessing your abilities. Think of these initial goals as stepping stones toward the greater challenges that lie ahead—your "mountains." By approaching your goals this way, you acknowledge that the journey itself is integral to your growth. Each step is not just progress but an opportunity for personal development and learning. This measured approach ensures that you grow steadily, gaining the necessary experience and confidence to tackle more significant challenges as you progress in your academic or career path.

Relevant: Ensure that the outcomes of your goals have significant value to you—be it personal growth, professional gain, or a tangible achievement. Choose objectives that lead to visible results that you can celebrate and take pride in. This tangible success validates your efforts and fuels your motivation to pursue further milestones. Make sure these goals resonate with your long-term visions and feel truly rewarding. Centering your goals around meaningful results enhances your engagement and commitment to the process. Each achievement should bring a sense of fulfillment and propel you toward your next target.

Time-Bound: Establish a clear timeline to achieve your goals; remember, procrastination is often our greatest adversary. Setting specific deadlines for yourself creates a structured framework that encourages consistent progress. Regularly monitor how well you adhere to these deadlines and assess the impact of each step on your ultimate objective. Developing a strong sense of time management is one of the most crucial skills you can cultivate. It helps you stay proactive and prepared for upcoming challenges, as well as demonstrates to others your respect and appreciation for your time and theirs. These small yet impactful habits are essential to building a foundation for success in your academic or professional life.

Breaking Down Large Goals into Manageable Tasks

To effectively manage your goals, it's crucial to approach them as significant tasks that require organization and strategic planning. Think of managing your academic and career objectives as taking on a part-time job that you schedule regularly and actively ensure effectiveness. Below are some insights on effective goal management that will help keep you on track.

Understand and Connect With Your Goal:

Take the time to deeply reflect on what achieving your goal truly means for you. Consider the implications it has on your life:

- **Assess its significance:** Is this goal a challenge that needs to be conquered? What concrete advantages can you expect from it?
- **Evaluate the commitment:** Understand how pursuing this goal will affect other areas of your life. What might you need to sacrifice or postpone to make room for this endeavor? Are these sacrifices temporary or long-term?
- **Prioritize appropriately:** Before diving in, ensure nothing more urgent requires your attention. It's important to address any pressing issues that might hinder your focus on your new goals.
- **Measure worth against effort:** Ensure that the goal is achievable and worth the effort. Reflect on whether the outcome will bring you satisfaction and if it aligns with your longer-term aspirations. This could involve considering the time, energy, and resources you need to invest in the goal, and whether the potential benefits outweigh these costs.

Split Your Goal Into Mini-Goals:

Attempting to tackle a large goal simultaneously can be daunting and may hinder your progress. To avoid feeling overwhelmed, break down your main goal into smaller, more manageable mini-goals. These steps should be clear, achievable, and systematically lead you toward achieving your larger goal. This division makes the task less intimidating and establishes a transparent system of achievement and reward, which can significantly boost your motivation.

For example, suppose your main goal is to write a thesis. Your mini-goals include outlining the thesis, conducting initial research, writing the first draft, revising, and final submission. Each step leads to the next, creating a structured path toward completion.

Create a List of Tasks:

For each mini-goal, create a detailed list of tasks. These lists should not only outline the necessary tasks but also incorporate potential challenges and strategies to overcome them. Consider adding reminders or tips that could make these tasks easier. This level of detail will help you approach your tasks more efficiently and effectively each time, turning what may initially seem daunting into a routine you can master.

For instance, if part of your goal involves learning a new software tool, your task list could include specific tutorials to watch, exercises to practice, and deadlines for mastering different tool functions.

Review Regularly:

Regular reviews are crucial to staying on track with your goals. By consistently evaluating your progress, you not only confirm that you are on the right path but also have the opportunity to adjust your strategies as needed. Think of this regular review as a way to actively manage your trajectory—similar to how you would approach a job or a passionate hobby. It's about taking control and ensuring every step is deliberate and aligned with your end goals.

During these reviews, ask yourself questions like:

- Am I progressing as planned?
- What challenges have I encountered, and how have I addressed them?
- Do any aspects of my plan need adjusting?

With these methods, you can maintain confidence and effectively navigate your path, adjusting as needed. By treating goal management as an integral part of your routine, you embed these practices into your daily life, paving the way for continued success and growth.

VISUALIZATION TECHNIQUES TO IMAGINE FUTURE SUCCESSES AND CREATE A ROADMAP

Visualization can enhance your ability to achieve academic and career goals. Forming a clear mental picture of what you want can boost your motivation and clarify the steps needed to succeed. This section will guide you through practical visualization exercises and encourage you to construct a detailed roadmap for your journey toward success.

Why Is Visualizing Important?

Visualization leverages the brain's capacity to simulate experiences, making it a vital tool for goal-setting and achievement. It helps solidify your commitment to your goals and enhances your ability to manifest them. By regularly visualizing your success, you embed these aspirations deeply within your subconscious, which can influence your daily decisions and actions towards achieving them.

Visualization is more than just wishful thinking; it's an essential step in skill acquisition and improving performance. Metcalf highlights the importance of this process, stating, "Imagining doing the thing contributes to you getting better at it—as long as you actually do the thing too." This practice embeds new neural patterns in the brain, effectively mapping paths to action. It's crucial that the mental rehearsal and the actual execution work together, ensuring that the envisioned activities translate into actual capabilities.

Visualization Techniques to Achieve Your Goals

1. **Create a Vision Board**: Compose images and words that represent your goals and aspirations on a vision board. This visual representation constantly reminds you of what you're working towards, keeping your objectives in mind.
2. **Write a Vision Statement**: Create a comprehensive vision statement that clearly articulates your desired achievements and ambitions. This statement should be inspiring and comprehensive, reflecting the end goal and the values driving it.

3. **Embrace Resources**: Utilize resources that align with your vision, such as books, podcasts, and seminars that can provide knowledge and inspiration relevant to your goals.

4. **Practice Journaling**: Keep a daily or weekly journal where you reflect on your progress and visualize future successes. This practice can help clarify your thoughts and solidify your commitment to your goals.

5. **Set Aside Time for Visualization Meditation**: Dedicate time daily or weekly to meditate on your goals. Use this quiet time to clearly imagine achieving your goals, including the emotions and experiences associated with success.

6. **Engage Specific Mental Imagery**: When visualizing, be as detailed as possible. Imagine the setting, the sounds, the conversations, and the emotions you'll feel when you reach your goals.

7. **Visualize a Plan and Take Action**: Beyond imagining the end result, visualize the steps required to get there. This includes foreseeing potential challenges and mentally rehearsing how you'll handle them.

8. **Get as Close to Your Vision as Possible**: Make your vision a part of your everyday life. If your goal is a new career, engage in activities related to that field. If it's academic success, create a study environment that mirrors your vision of an ideal learning space.

Using Totems and Rituals

Another creative visualization technique involves using totems and rituals—physical items or actions that symbolically represent your goals. These can serve as tangible reminders of what you're working towards. For instance, wearing a specific color on days you're focused on a particular goal, or carrying a token that represents your aspirations, like a keyring for the keys to a new home you're saving for. Each interaction with these totems can reinforce your commitment and refocus your efforts.

Integrating these visualization techniques into your routine can enhance your ability to achieve your goals. Whether through creative visual aids, structured planning, or symbolic totems, each strategy offers a unique way to keep your aspirations vivid and within reach.

Vision Board

Crafted with intention, a vision board transforms your aspirations into a tangible, inspiring work of art. It is more than just a collection of pictures. Instead, it is a continual prompt of your leadership goals and steadfast dedication to making a beneficial difference in your society. By visualizing your goals, you are more likely to stay inspired and maintain focus on your objectives.

Creating Your Vision Board:

1. Gather Materials:

- If you prefer an electronic version, a large poster board, or a digital platform.

- Magazines, newspapers, or printed images.
- You will need scissors, glue, markers, and other decorative items.

2. Define Your Goals:

- Reflect on your aspirations related to leadership and community impact.
- Consider what leadership means to you, as well as how you want to contribute to your community.

3. Find Inspiration:

- Search for images, quotes, and affirmations that resonate with your goals.
- Look for visuals representing the qualities of leadership you admire and the impact you wish to have in your community.

4. Layout and Design:

- Arrange your materials on the board in an organized and inspiring way.
- Group similar themes together to give your board a cohesive look and feel.

5. Prompts to Get Started:

- Choose a quote that defines your philosophy on leadership.
- Select images of leaders who inspire you.

- Write or find affirmations that strengthen your resolve to serve and lead.
- Include visuals that represent your community and the changes you hope to enact.

6. Personal Touch:

- Add personal photos or mementos that remind you of your journey and why you're committed to your goals.
- Consider using colors or symbols that have personal significance.

7. Use the Board:

- Place your vision board somewhere you will see it daily—next to your mirror, above your desk, or as a wallpaper on your device.
- Let it be a daily inspiration and a guide as you work towards your goals.

Benefits of a Vision Board:

- Keep your goals visible and at the forefront of your mind.
- Inspires daily motivation and positive action.
- Helps clarify and concentrate your efforts on your most important aspirations.

Goal-Setting Worksheet

Here is a worksheet for setting your academic and career goals and milestones using the SMART framework.

Goal Setting Worksheet
Outline your goal in detail:
How will you measure your success?
Is your goal attainable? Yes / No
How is the goal relevant to you? Your community?
How long will you give yourself to complete the goal?
Short Term Goals:
Long Term Goals:
Write down the steps to get to your goal: 1.   2.   3.
Remember to check in regularly. Record your check-in dates below for accuracy.

Final Thoughts

As we wrap up this chapter, let's reflect on the empowering tools and insights we've explored to drive your academic and career success. You've learned how affirmations can elevate your mindset, boosting confidence, motivation, and focus. By adopting SMART goal-setting strategies, you can break your grand aspirations into achievable tasks. Moreover, the visualization techniques introduced will serve as a roadmap, guiding you through each step toward your envisioned future.

Now, it's time to take these tools and implement them. Reinforce your affirmations daily, refine your goals regularly, and visualize your success frequently. Each step you take is a building block towards your ultimate achievements.

Looking ahead, remember that while individual success is thrilling, the relationships you nurture make the journey even more rewarding. In the next chapter, we'll delve into how cultivating healthy relationships and effective communication can enrich your life and amplify your successes. These skills will bolster your personal and professional growth, laying the foundation for lasting achievements. Let's continue building on what you've learned and prepare to enhance the connections surrounding you.

CULTIVATING HEALTHY RELATIONSHIPS AND EFFECTIVE COMMUNICATION

When you look at the people around you, do you ever consider how they affect your success or how you affect theirs? Are you having a positive impact on each other? How could you improve your relationships to be more supportive of both parties?

As digital interactions continue to replace or overshadow face-to-face connections, understanding the nuances of effective communication and the value of supportive relationships is more important than ever. This chapter delves into why healthy relationships matter, how they shape our experiences and self-perception, and why effective communication is critical to maintaining them. From mastering the art of listening to expressing empathy and understanding non-verbal cues, you'll learn how to enhance your interactions and foster a network that supports your journey toward personal and professional success.

Whether navigating friendships, mentoring relationships, or family dynamics, the skills and knowledge you gain from this chapter will help you create a foundation of solid and supportive relationships. You'll discover practical exercises to improve your listening skills, engage more deeply in conversations, and understand others' perspectives more fully. The design of each section builds on the previous one, offering a comprehensive toolkit that will serve you well beyond your teenage years.

THE IMPORTANCE OF HEALTHY RELATIONSHIPS AND POSITIVE SOCIAL CIRCLES

Maintaining healthy and positive relationships has a big impact on your self-esteem, mental health, and personal growth. When you have relationships based on mutual respect and understanding, it improves your emotional well-being and helps you stay physically healthy. These relationships also support you in achieving your goals.

Mental Health

The quality of our relationships can directly influence our physical and mental health. Engaging in healthy relationships where positivity prevails can reduce symptoms of depression and anxiety and bolster our overall resilience. For instance, individuals in supportive social environments often experience quicker recovery from illnesses and feel more emotionally balanced. On the other hand, both mental and physical health can suffer from loneliness and social isolation, negatively impacting our well-being and energy. According to research by Michelle A. Harris and Ulrich Orth, positive social interactions and acceptance play crucial roles in the development of self-esteem across all ages, from childhood through old age (Harris, 2019). Establishing and nurturing these relationships early in life not only promotes better health but also sets a foundation for lifelong personal empowerment and motivation.

Self Esteem

Feeling accepted and valued within your social circle can significantly boost your self-esteem. The satisfaction of being heard and respected, as well as knowing that your words impact others, instills a deep sense of confidence. These interactions teach us the importance of admiration, appreciation, and love while giving us the opportunity to reciprocate these positive feelings. Conversely, low self-esteem and superficial relationships can lead to negative emotional spirals, diminishing your sense of self-worth and negatively affecting your attitude toward life and personal goals.

Impact on Personal Growth

Healthy relationships are a cornerstone of personal growth. They provide a safe space to experiment with new ideas, confront challenges, and gain feedback without fear of judgment. This supportive environment encourages risk-taking and innovation, essential components of personal and professional development. Furthermore, a robust social network can unlock new opportunities, offering personal and professional benefits that foster growth and achievement.

Healthy relationships and cultivating a positive social circle are integral to your overall well-being. They not only enhance your self-esteem and personal growth but also contribute to improved mental and physical health, forming a positive cycle that supports your life aspirations. As you continue to invest in your relationships, remember that each positive interaction is a step towards building a more fulfilling and successful life.

Courage Through Companionship: A Look at Supportive Friends and Mentors

Achieving greatness often isn't a solo journey; behind many successful individuals are the mentors and friends who have provided essential support along the way. Understanding the value of these relationships can help us seek out and nurture such connections in our lives, as well as learn how to be better friends and mentors to others.

The Power of Mentorship in the Black Community

Mentorship is pivotal in fostering social and academic success, particularly within the Black community. A recent study highlighted the significant impact of mentorship programs, revealing that 95% of mentored Black youth completed high school, and 82% pursued further education or vocational training (Lee, 2023). These statistics underscore the transformative power of having guidance and support from those who have navigated similar paths and challenges.

Real-Life Impact: Mentor of the Year

The importance of mentorship is personified in the story of an individual recently honored as 'Mentor of the Year' for his dedication to mentoring young Black boys. His journey into mentorship was profoundly influenced by his aunt, who was his first mentor. Her unwavering love and support, combined with the guidance of a Black male mentor, shaped his mentoring approach, allowing him to pass on the legacy of positive influence (Deaderick, 2023). His story is a testament to the ripple effect of mentorship—how one supportive relationship can inspire an individual to impact many.

Affirmations for Respect, Empathy, and Understanding in Interactions

Cultivating a mindset of respect, empathy, and understanding is foundational to building and maintaining supportive relationships. Affirmations can be crucial in fostering these qualities, enhancing our interactions with others, and strengthening our connections.

Affirmations can significantly influence how we perceive and interact with the world around us, especially when building and maintaining healthy relationships. Fostering a mindset grounded in respect, empathy, and understanding can enhance our interactions and strengthen our connections. Here, we explore two scenarios where such affirmations can nurture positive relationships.

Scenario 1: Navigating New Friendships

Title: Bridging Worlds

First-Person Perspective: I recently moved to a new city for college, which meant leaving behind my close-knit group of friends. I felt an overwhelming urge to fit in and make new friends at my new university, but I was anxious about the reception I would receive. Would I find people who shared my interests and values, or would I have to change to feel accepted?

During the first week, I met Alex, who invited me to join a study group. I was excited but nervous; these were potential new friends from diverse backgrounds. I remembered an affirmation I started practicing: "I am open and ready to connect with others, and I bring value to every interaction."

Effect on Belief System: This affirmation helped me approach the study group with confidence and an open heart. Instead of worrying about being judged, I focused on being present and getting to know each person. I listened actively and shared my thoughts without fear, which not only made me feel more connected but also helped me realize that genuine friendships could blossom from mutual respect and understanding.

Positive Affirmations:

- "I am worthy of meaningful friendships that respect and celebrate my true self."
- "Every person I meet brings a new perspective that enriches my understanding."

- "I contribute positively to my interactions, making them enjoyable and worthwhile."

Reaffirmed Belief System: These affirmations strengthened my resolve to engage openly in new relationships, emphasizing the importance of being myself. They reassured me that respect and empathy are reciprocal; by offering them, I invite them back into my life, fostering deeper and more meaningful connections.

Scenario 2: Overcoming Misunderstandings

Title: Clearing the Air

First-Person Perspective: At work, I found myself involved in a misunderstanding with a colleague, Sarah, over project responsibilities. Tensions were high, and there was an air of frustration between us. Prior to our project discussion meeting, I concentrated on the affirmation, "I strive to comprehend before gaining understanding."

Effect on Belief System: This mindset shift was crucial. It allowed me to enter the conversation to understand Sarah's perspective rather than defend my own. By doing so, I could empathize with her concerns and collaboratively find a solution that acknowledged our strengths.

Positive Affirmations:

- "I approach conflicts with an open mind and a heart ready to understand."
- "My willingness to listen and empathize strengthens my relationships."

- "I am a bridge-builder; I turn conflicts into opportunities for growth and connection."

Reaffirmed Belief System: These affirmations enabled me to transform a potentially divisive situation into one that enhanced mutual respect and cooperation. By valuing empathy and striving for understanding, I resolved the immediate issue. I laid the groundwork for a more collaborative relationship moving forward.

In both scenarios, affirmations of respect, empathy, and understanding play a pivotal role in shaping constructive and supportive interactions. Whether forming new friendships or navigating conflicts, these affirmations encourage a compassionate approach that can lead to deeper connections and more fulfilling relationships. Below are a few more affirmations to shape and make your own.

Affirmations for Better Relationships

1. **"I treat others with respect and value their unique perspectives."**

   - Use this affirmation to remind yourself to approach every interaction respectfully and to recognize the inherent worth of others' views and experiences.

2. **"I listen with empathy and strive to understand the feelings and experiences of others."**

   - This affirmation encourages active listening and empathy, which are essential for deepening relationships and fostering mutual understanding.

3. "I am open to learning from everyone I meet, recognizing that everyone has something valuable to teach me."

- Embrace this mindset to maintain humility and openness in your interactions, which is vital when seeking guidance from mentors or peers.

4. "I give back to those who guide me, sharing my appreciation and support freely."

- Affirm your commitment to reciprocity in all relationships, ensuring that you are taking advice and giving back in meaningful ways.

5. "I nurture my relationships with care and dedication, celebrating our shared successes."

- Use this affirmation to keep you engaged in actively maintaining and appreciating your relationships, recognizing that they require ongoing effort and celebration.

6. "I am committed to becoming someone who others can look up to and depend on."

- This affirmation supports becoming a mentor, fostering a cycle of positivity and empowerment in your community.

The Role of Affirmations in Enhancing Personal Interactions

Implementing these affirmations can significantly impact your daily interactions and overall approach to building relationships:

- **Enhancing Empathy**: Regularly reciting affirmations focusing on empathy and understanding helps internalize these attitudes, making them more natural in your interactions.
- **Building Respect**: Affirmations emphasizing respect ensure that it remains a core value in all your relationships, promoting environments where everyone feels valued and heard.
- **Encouraging Reciprocity**: By affirming the importance of mutual support, you foster balanced and enriching relationships for all parties involved.
- **Supporting Personal Growth**: As you practice these affirmations, you not only improve your interactions but also develop qualities that make you a better friend, mentor, and community member.

These affirmations reinforce the behaviors and attitudes that are essential for developing supportive, empathetic, and respectful relationships. These affirmations remind you of your role in creating and sustaining positive interactions, ultimately leading to stronger connections and a more supportive community.

EXERCISES TO ENHANCE COMMUNICATION SKILLS AND SOCIAL INTELLIGENCE

Your listening skills are on notice, as are the rest of ours. It takes practice to be a good listener. As the pace of information flow accelerates in our digital world, we often adapt to receiving data quickly, akin to instantaneous search engine results. This shift can inadvertently affect how we handle personal interactions, where the tempo of information exchange is slower and more nuanced. Unlike a quick search online, human communication requires us to give others the time and space to articulate complex ideas and emotions effectively. People need to express themselves without rushing, which fosters a sense of openness and trust in conversations. Please find below some activities to help you improve these skills.

Exercises to Improve Listening Skills

Improving communication involves several vital practices that enhance listening, speaking, and interpreting non-verbal cues. Here are some steps to practice more effective communication:

Balancing Listening With Verbal and Non-Verbal Communication Skills

Slowing Down in Conversations: Give your full attention to validating others' feelings and thoughts, allowing them to articulate their ideas fully. This respectful approach ensures you understand their intentions and emotions, recognizing the human aspect of interaction.

Verbal Communication: Make your contributions to conversations thoughtful and meaningful. Reflect on what has been said and provide insights or support that advance the dialogue, demonstrating your engagement and concern for the discussion.

Non-Verbal Cues: The act of communicating goes beyond the use of words and encompasses nonverbal cues such as body language, facial expressions, and tone of voice. Paying attention to these cues offers deeper insights into others' feelings, helping you respond more empathetically and appropriately.

Observing Subtleties: Be attentive to the other person's non-verbal signals, which can reveal emotions that words might not. Recognizing these cues enhances your understanding of their perspective and guides your responses to acknowledge their true feelings.

Mindfulness in Interaction: Engage fully in every interaction by being present, listening intently, and observing without judgment. This approach fosters more meaningful relationships and ensures that communication is reciprocal and enriching, making everyone involved feel heard, understood, and valued.

Active Listening Techniques

- **Summarize What You Hear:** Show you are processing information by summarizing others' points.
- **Ask Open-ended Questions:** Foster deeper dialogue with questions that require more than yes/no answers.

- **Provide Feedback:** Offer thoughtful feedback that reflects your understanding of the discussion.
- **Listen Without Interrupting:** Challenge yourself to fully listen without interjecting, enhancing your understanding of the speaker's intent and emotions.
- **Voice Blogging:** Start a voice blog to discuss topics of interest, practice clear articulation, and offer a platform for vocal expression.
- **Listen for the Hidden Phrase:** Focus on identifying key phrases or underlying messages in conversations or recordings to boost concentration and depth of understanding.

Role-Playing Scenarios to Encourage Empathy

- **Placing the Celebrity:** Discuss how a celebrity might react in everyday situations to explore different communication styles and perspectives.
- **Stand Up/Sit Down Workout:** Engage in an activity where participants express their stance on statements, then discuss the reasons behind their choices, promoting an appreciation for diverse viewpoints.
- **Vowel Discrimination:** Enhance auditory discrimination skills by identifying words with similar vowel sounds but different meanings, improving your ability to distinguish nuances in spoken communication.

These structured exercises are designed to improve your communication skills by enhancing your listening abilities, empathy, and responsiveness. Practicing these techniques will lead to better personal and professional relationships and a deeper understanding of those around you.

Relationship Exercises

Understanding and improving your relationships begins with self-reflection. This section offers guided exercises to help you explore your current relationships; journal prompts to enhance your expression of thoughts and feelings, and practical scenarios to develop your listening and empathy skills. These tools foster deeper self-awareness and more meaningful connections with others.

Guided Exercises for Self-Reflection on Current Relationships:

Relationship Mapping:

1. **Objective:** Identify and evaluate the nature and impact of your relationships.
2. **Exercise:** Draw a map, placing yourself at the center. Surround your image with circles representing critical people in your life. Draw lines connecting you to each person. Use different line styles to represent the nature of each relationship (solid, dashed, thick, or thin), reflecting closeness, positivity, and support.
3. **Reflection:** Which relationships provide support? Which ones need more attention or boundary setting?

Gratitude Reflection:

1. **Objective:** Acknowledge and appreciate positive relationships.
2. **Exercise:** List at least three people for whom you are grateful. Write down why you are grateful for each person and how they impact your life positively.
3. **Reflection:** How do expressions of gratitude enhance these relationships?

Journal Prompts to Practice Expressing Thoughts and Feelings:

- "Today, I felt misunderstood by someone. Here's what happened and how I wish I could have expressed myself..."
- "A recent conflict that I could have handled better was... Here are the thoughts and feelings I wish I had shared..."
- "One thing I admire about someone in my life is... Here's why I feel this way and haven't told them..."

Tips for Effective Journaling:

- Be honest and open with your feelings.
- Use writing as a tool to explore and clarify your emotions.
- Regularly revisit your entries to observe patterns and growth over time.

Scenarios for Developing Listening and Empathy Skills:

Scenario 1: Misunderstood Friend

1. **Context:** Your friend is upset after receiving criticism at work and vents to you.
2. **Task:** Practice active listening by summarizing their feelings, asking open-ended questions to delve deeper, and expressing empathy without offering unsolicited advice.
3. **Reflection:** How did your response affect the conversation? Did your friend feel heard and supported?

Scenario 2: Family Conflict

1. **Context:** A family member is angry about plans that went awry, which also impacted you.
2. **Task:** Use empathic listening to acknowledge their feelings and perspectives, even if you disagree. Discuss your feelings using "I" statements to express your viewpoint without blame.
3. **Reflection:** How did addressing both perspectives help resolve the conflict?

Final Thoughts

In this chapter, we delved into the fundamentals of building and maintaining strong, healthy relationships and the importance of effective communication. We explored various techniques and exercises designed to enhance your self-awareness, improve your listening skills, and foster empathy. We gave examples of individuals who've prospered from healthy community relationships and crafted affirmations to aid you in your endeavors. These tools are essential for developing deeper connections with those around you and navigating interpersonal challenges with grace and understanding.

I encourage you to put these ideas into practice. Reflect on your current relationships using the guided exercises, express your thoughts and feelings through the journal prompts provided, and engage in the scenarios to hone your listening and empathy skills.

Looking ahead, we will turn our focus inward. The next chapter is dedicated to embracing a holistic approach to your health and wellness. You've learned how to nurture your relationships and communication; now it's time to ensure you are taking care of your entire being—mind, body, and spirit. We will explore strategies to integrate physical activity, mental health practices, and spiritual growth into your daily life, helping you build a strong, resilient foundation for all aspects of your life. Get ready to transform how you live and thrive each day!

A HOLISTIC APPROACH TO
HEALTH AND WELLNESS

U nderstanding the interconnectedness of your physical
and mental well-being aids in driving success in all
areas of your life. Like an engine and its driver, each component relies on the other to function optimally. Recognizing
this relationship is the first step towards a more balanced
and healthier lifestyle.

INTEGRATING AFFIRMATIONS WITH PHYSICAL
WELLNESS

Integrating affirmations with physical wellness transcends
the mere act of exercising; it involves embedding a mental
resilience that amplifies the efficacy of physical efforts.
Combining affirmations with physical activity not only
promotes regular participation but also transforms the exercise into a source of strength, both mentally and physically.

Integrating affirmations into your workout routine starts with setting the right tone before each session. For instance, affirmations like "Every step I take builds my strength and confidence" or "I am energized by my ability to push my limits" can prepare your mind to engage fully in the workout ahead. This mental preparation increases your stamina and endurance during physical activity. It helps you approach each session with enthusiasm and determination.

Affirmations play a crucial role in countering the negative self-talk that often arises during challenging physical tasks. When your body starts to feel fatigue or discomfort, affirmations like "I am powerful; I am relentless" or "My body is capable of amazing things" can shift your focus from discomfort to capability. This shift not only eases the perception of pain but also boosts your overall exercise performance by reinforcing a positive mindset, making you feel more resilient and capable.

The benefits of combining affirmations with physical wellness go beyond the workout itself. After your exercise, affirmations can be used to solidify your sense of accomplishment and foster regular exercise habits. Phrases like "I am proud of myself for showing up today" or "I honor my body with movement" help strengthen the link between physical activity and self-respect, motivating you to maintain a sustainable routine and feel more accomplished.

Scenario 1: Starting a New Fitness Regimen

Title: New Beginnings

First-Person Perspective: I've always known the importance of staying active, but lately, I have felt unmotivated. The idea of starting a new fitness regimen seemed daunting. Then, I decided to pair my workouts with affirmations. As I laced up my running shoes each morning, I repeated, "Moving my body brings balance to my emotions." This simple mantra helped me view exercise as an act of self-love rather than a chore.

Effect on Belief System: This affirmation transformed my outlook. No longer was I exercising to meet physical goals; I was also nurturing my mental health. The affirmation reminded me that each step was improving my mood and resilience. The mental clarity and stress relief that followed each workout became my motivation.

Positive Affirmations for Starting a New Fitness Regimen:

- "Exercise is loving my body and the greatest gift I can give myself."
- "The pain of today's workout makes me stronger for tomorrow."
- "I am coordinated and athletic."
- "Every time I show up for my workout, I affirm my worthiness."

Scenario 2: Overcoming Workout Plateaus

Title: Pushing Through

First-Person Perspective: Hitting a plateau can be frustrating. Recently, I found myself losing interest in my workouts and feeling like I wasn't making progress. Then, I started using the affirmation, "Without challenge, there's no change!" whenever I felt like skipping a workout or giving up halfway through.

Effect on Belief System: This powerful statement rekindled my drive. It reminded me that overcoming this plateau was another hurdle on my fitness journey, crucial for growth. Each session felt like a step closer to a breakthrough, and I learned to embrace the challenges as opportunities for growth.

Positive Affirmations for Overcoming Workout Plateaus:

- "My body loves me and supports my goals."
- "The stronger I am in body, the stronger I become mentally."
- "I have never regretted a workout!"
- "It's time to move; I'll rest later."

How to Use Your Workout Affirmations

There are several ways to incorporate affirmations into your workout routine to stay motivated and focused:

- **During Warm-ups and Cool-downs:** Use affirmations to set the tone for your workout or to wind down with positive thoughts.
- **Between Reps:** Repeat your affirmations between sets to maintain a high energy level.
- **En Route to the Gym:** Start your mental preparation on the way to your workout by repeating affirmations that gear you up for a great session.
- **Through Visual Reminders:** Post affirmations on your bathroom mirror, add them as reminders on your phone, or print and frame them in your workout area.
- **As Meditation Mantras:** Incorporate affirmations into your meditation practice can help you connect better with your physical and mental goals.

Combining these practical uses of affirmations with physical activity enhances your mental resilience and physical strength.

MENTAL AND EMOTIONAL HEALTH

Just as physical fitness is important, maintaining a balance between mental and emotional health is equally crucial. In this section, we will delve into practical strategies for managing stress and anxiety that have been proven to lead to improved well-being and an improved quality of life. Research demonstrates that these methods, such as breathing exercises, mindfulness practices, and meditation, not only alleviate symptoms and promote relaxation by inducing a sense of peace but also instill confidence in their effectiveness.

Breathing Techniques for Stress Relief

Breathing exercises are powerful techniques that can reduce stress, anxiety, and tension while calming your mind and improving focus.

- **Abdominal Breathing:** This involves focusing on deep, even breaths from your diaphragm, which increases oxygen flow and promotes a sense of calm. Practice this technique by placing one hand on your belly and another on your chest, ensuring your belly rises more than yours as you breathe.
- **Guided Breathing Exercises:** These are especially helpful if you are new to breathing techniques. Many apps and online videos can guide you through paced breathing exercises designed to reduce anxiety.

Mindfulness Exercises to Reduce Stress

Mindfulness involves being fully present in the moment, aware of where we are and what we're doing, without being overly reactive or overwhelmed by what's happening around us.

- **Meditative Walking (Core Walking):** This practice involves walking slowly and deliberately, focusing on each movement and the sensation of your feet touching the ground. You can practice it anywhere, whether it's on a quiet path or a bustling city street.

- **Drinking a Cup of Tea:** Engage fully in the experience of making and sipping tea. Notice the aroma, the heat, and the taste as you slowly drink, allowing yourself to be present and relaxed.
- **Connecting With Nature:** Activities like hiking or spending time in a garden can help you connect with the environment and ground your thoughts.
- **Gazing Meditation:** Focus on a single point or object. This could be a candle flame, a spot on the wall, or a distant tree. The act of focused gazing helps clear the mind of clutter.

Guided Meditation and Stretching

- **Guided Meditation:** These sessions are led by an instructor, either in person or via a recording. They can help you navigate stress and reach deep relaxation and mindfulness.
- **Stretching:** Regular stretching exercises can release muscle tension and promote relaxation. Combine this with deep breathing to enhance the stress-relieving effects.

Implementing These Practices

By seamlessly incorporating these techniques into your daily routine, you can effectively manage your stress and anxiety. To ease into it, start with small steps, such as a five-minute breathing exercise or a short walk, and gradually lengthen the time as you feel more comfortable. Remember, the key to mastering these practices is consistency and mindfulness, which empowers you to manage your stress and anxiety effectively.

THE ART OF MINDFULNESS: RELIEF AND CLARITY THROUGH MINDFUL TECHNIQUES

Mindfulness involves fully embracing each moment, tuning into the sensations around us, and appreciating the subtle details of life that often go unnoticed. It is a form of art that encourages you to pause, reflect on your immediate environment, and engage deeply with your thoughts, emotions, and physical sensations. This practice helps you connect with your surroundings and serves as a revitalizing break, offering moments of peace and clarity that can enhance your daily life.

Scientific studies highlight the potential benefits of mindfulness, particularly within African American communities, which statistically face elevated levels of chronic stress. Implementing mindfulness practices in these communities could significantly mitigate stress and improve overall health outcomes (Biggers et al., 2020).

One impactful initiative is Black Girls Breathing, founded by Jasmine Marie. This organization offers specialized meditational breathwork sessions designed for Black women and girls, aiming to address and alleviate the unique stressors prevalent within the Black community. The growing participation in these sessions reflects their positive impact, showcasing how mindfulness can effectively engage and support community well-being (Kindelan, 2021).

Developing a Mindfulness Practice

To fully realize the benefits of mindfulness, such as enhanced calm and mental clarity, it's essential to develop a routine that suits your personal needs. Consistency in practice can dramatically improve your ability to manage stress, sharpen your focus, and enhance your overall well-being. Below are some fundamental mindfulness techniques and the specific benefits they can bring to your routine.

Practice Having Empathy for Others

Technique: Engage actively in listening to others without judgment, trying to truly understand their perspective and emotions.

Improves: This practice enhances your emotional intelligence and strengthens relationships. It also helps in reducing personal biases and enhancing social interactions.

Breathing Exercises

Technique: Incorporate deep, controlled breathing exercises into your daily routine. This can involve techniques like the 4-7-8 method or diaphragmatic breathing.

Improves: Regular breathing exercises increase oxygen flow, reduce anxiety, and stabilize blood pressure. They can also help maintain emotional balance during stressful situations.

Spend Some Time Outside Without Your Phone

Technique: Take regular walks in nature or sit in a park without any digital distractions.

Improves: This activity reduces symptoms of stress and anxiety, boosts mood, and enhances creativity. It provides a break from constant connectivity, allowing for a mental reset.

Journal

Technique: Keep a daily journal where you express your thoughts, feelings, and daily experiences.

Improves: Journaling aids in self-reflection and emotional expression, promotes problem-solving, and can act as a tool for better mental health by clarifying thoughts and tracking day-to-day patterns.

Take Pauses for Observation

Technique: Throughout your day, take brief moments to pause and fully observe your surroundings or internal state without any judgment.

Improves: This helps in developing presence and mindfulness, reducing the tendency to operate on autopilot, and increasing appreciation for small details in daily life.

Doodle or Freewrite

Technique: Allow yourself sessions of freeform drawing or writing where there is no pressure to produce something specific or functional.

Improves: This boosts creative expression and problem-solving abilities, reduces stress, and can offer insight into your subconscious thoughts and feelings.

Tips for Implementing Your Mindfulness Routine

1. **Set Specific Times:** Dedicate specific times of the day for your mindfulness practices to help turn them into habits.
2. **Create a Mindful Environment:** Arrange a dedicated space in your home where you can practice these activities undisturbed.
3. **Be Patient and Persistent:** Mindfulness is a skill that develops over time, so give yourself the grace to grow into these practices without expecting immediate perfection.
4. **Regular Reflection:** Periodically assess what is working and what isn't, and feel free to adjust your techniques to better suit your evolving needs.

DAILY ROUTINES FOR WELLNESS

Creating a balanced daily routine that incorporates affirmations, meditation, and physical activity can significantly enhance your overall wellness. Establishing a personalized and manageable routine can transform these practices from daunting tasks to enjoyable parts of your day, ultimately fostering both mental and physical health.

Practical Tips for Crafting Your Wellness Routine

Incorporate Daily Affirmations: Affirmations are powerful tools for fostering a positive mindset and can set the tone for your day. Start your morning by stating affirmations that resonate with your goals and aspirations. Place affirmation cards around your mirror, desk, or anywhere you'll see them regularly to remind yourself of your worth and capabilities.

Meditation Practices: Integrating meditation into your daily routine can help reduce stress and improve concentration. Start with just a few minutes each day. Use guided sessions from apps or online platforms if beginning on your own feels overwhelming. Establish a specific spot in your home for meditation to create a dedicated space for mindfulness activities.

Physical Activity: Exercise doesn't have to be confined to the gym. Integrate physical activity into your daily routine by maximizing daily tasks:

- **Household Tasks as Exercise:** Turn cleaning, gardening, or even cooking into mini-workouts by incorporating stretches, squats, or balancing exercises.
- **Active TV Time:** Use TV time to get moving. Try exercises like jumping jacks or sit-ups during commercial breaks, or invest in a stationary bike or treadmill if space permits.

- **Work Routine Integration:** If you work at a desk, set reminders to stand, stretch, or do brief exercises every hour. If possible, opt for walking meetings or use part of your lunch break for a short walk.
- **Choosing the Stairs:** Whenever possible, opt for the stairs over elevators or escalators to increase your daily step count and boost cardiovascular health.

Making Wellness Enjoyable: The secret to sticking with a wellness routine is ensuring it's enjoyable and tailored to your preferences. When you integrate activities you love and find ways to make less exciting tasks more enjoyable, your routine becomes less of a chore and more of a rewarding part of your daily life.

Customizing Your Routine with Enjoyable Activities

Incorporate Passions into Exercise: If traditional workouts don't excite you, think outside the box. For instance, if you love dancing, include dance workouts in your routine. This switch can inject an element of fun and keep you consistently engaged.

Pair Tasks with Pleasures: Align less enjoyable tasks with something you look forward to. For example, if stretching seems tedious, try doing it in front of your favorite TV show or listening to a captivating podcast or audiobook. This pairing can transform a mundane activity into a more pleasant experience, making it easier to commit to your wellness goals.

ENHANCING MOTIVATION THROUGH ENJOYMENT

Integrate Variety: Avoid routine fatigue by mixing different activities. Incorporating variety in activities not only helps in avoiding monotony but also engages different muscle groups and cognitive functions, which in turn improves both physical and mental health.

Set Achievable Goals: Motivation thrives on success. Set small, achievable goals within your routine to provide a sense of accomplishment. For example, aim to improve your dance moves or extend your stretching duration while enjoying an episode of a show.

Social Interaction: Whenever possible, involve friends or family in your wellness activities. Whether it's a dance class, a jogging session, or a joint stretching routine during a movie night, doing activities together can increase enjoyment and commitment.

WEAVING WELLNESS INTO DAILY LIFE

Routine Integration: Seamlessly integrate these activities into your daily schedule. Consistency is crucial, and by making your wellness activities a regular part of your day, you ensure they contribute to your holistic health.

Reflect and Adjust: Regularly assess what aspects of your routine are most enjoyable and effective. Don't hesitate to adjust or swap out activities to better suit your evolving interests and needs. This flexibility can keep your routine fresh and aligned with your personal growth.

Build Your Wellness Plan

Your Weekly Wellness Plan serves as a structured guide to help you maintain balance, achieve your fitness goals, and foster mental clarity throughout your week. This planner is about tracking your physical activities and reflecting on your mental and emotional growth. We've designed it to assist you in acknowledging minor achievements and pinpointing opportunities for enhancement in your everyday life.

You can document your physical activities, affirmations, and reflections each day. This consistent practice is a powerful tool in developing a deeper understanding of your interactions, achievements, and the emotions that shape your days. Whether it's a brisk walk, a yoga session, or a moment of deep breathing, make sure to note it down.

At the end of each week, you'll reflect on your overall progress, focusing on mindfulness activities. This is your time to observe the patterns in your thoughts and behaviors, learn from them, and plan how you can further enhance your upcoming week.

With a plan in hand, embrace the journey of self-improvement as you align your daily actions with your long-term wellness goals. Start each day with a clear intention and end with gratitude.

Weekly Wellness Plan Date:

Weekly Goals:

Motivations/notes from last week:

What will you improve from last week? How?

Day/Date:

Physical Activity/Time:

Affirmations:

Reflections:

Positive notes on today:

Encouragements for tomorrow:

Day/Date:

Physical Activity/Time:

Affirmations:

Reflections:

Positive notes on today:

Encouragements for tomorrow:

Day/Date:

Physical Activity/Time:

Affirmations:

Reflections:

Positive notes on today:

Encouragements for tomorrow:

Midweek Meditation and Mindfulness

Mindfulness activity/time:

Reflections:

Day/Date:

Physical Activity/Time:

Affirmations:

Reflections:

Positive notes on today:

Encouragements for tomorrow:

Day/Date:

Physical Activity/Time:

Affirmations:

Reflections:

Positive notes on today:

Encouragements for tomorrow:

Day/Date:

Physical Activity/Time:

Affirmations:

Reflections:

Positive notes on today:

Encouragements for tomorrow:

Day/Date:

Physical Activity/Time:

Affirmations:

Reflections:

Positive notes on today:

Encouragements for tomorrow:

Weekend Meditation and Mindfulness

Mindfulness activity/time:

Weekly Reflections:

What affirmations worked best for you, and why?

Did the midweek meditation yield any positive results?

How did you feel after your physical activities?

Do you plan to push harder or slow down a bit next week?

Affirmations/notes/suggestions for next week or take some time to free write:

Final Thoughts

Throughout this chapter, we've delved into the comprehensive nature of health, embracing the physical, mental, and emotional dimensions. By understanding the symbiotic relationship between mind and body, you've gained valuable insights into how to weave affirmations, exercise, and mindfulness into the fabric of your daily life. Your role in this journey is crucial, and your efforts are what will make a difference.

We explored the transformative power of combining physical activity with motivational affirmations to enhance mental health and overall motivation. We designed the strategies and exercises to be simple yet effective, enabling you to integrate them into your routine, whether at home or in your local community. This integration aims to build a regular practice that strengthens your body and elevates your spirit.

Additionally, the chapter highlighted various techniques to manage stress and anxiety, from breathing exercises to mindfulness and meditation. These tools are beneficial not only for personal growth but also for enhancing interactions and relationships with others.

As you apply the ideas presented in this chapter, remember that the journey to holistic health is a personal and ongoing process. Each step you take is not just a step but an investment in a healthier, more empowered version of yourself.

In the next chapter, we'll shift our focus from internal balance to external achievements. We'll explore how to channel your balanced energy and clarity into pursuing your dreams and mapping out a practical path to reach them. Get ready to dream big and learn the strategic steps necessary to realize those dreams.

PURSUING DREAMS AND
SETTING THE PATH FORWARD

A young girl from Texas lived in a segregated, rural town in the early 20th century. Despite facing racial and gender prejudice, she dreamed of flying high in the skies. This girl was Bessie Coleman, a person of remarkable resilience and determination. In Atlanta, Texas, on January 26, 1892, she came into the world as part of a sharecropping family. The racial segregation of the time only compounded the economic difficulties they already faced. Undeterred by the seemingly insurmountable obstacles, she harbored a dream that transcended the limits placed upon her by society: To take to the skies and become a pilot.

Despite the era's severe restrictions on both her race and gender, Coleman's ambition to fly was unshakeable. She knew that no American flight schools would admit her, so she saved her earnings and learned French to pursue aviation training in France. Her relentless pursuit paid off, and Bessie Coleman became the first African American woman to hold an international pilot's license, a shining example of extraordinary courage and resilience that can inspire us all.

Bessie Coleman's story is a powerful testament to the profound impact of maintaining a vision and the resilience required to achieve it, even when faced with overwhelming odds. As we delve into the principles of affirmations and goal-setting in this chapter, let her remarkable journey inspire you to set your sights high and work tirelessly towards your dreams. This section will provide you with practical guidance on how to use affirmations effectively to fuel your ambitions, equipping you with practical goal-setting strategies that create actionable plans to reach your aspirations. Additionally, we'll explore the importance of embracing failure as an integral part of personal growth, enhancing your ability to recover from setbacks and persist in the face of challenges.

AFFIRMATIONS TO INSPIRE AMBITION AND THE PURSUIT OF DREAMS

Your personal drive and determination primarily fuel the journey towards achieving your dreams. Along the way, you may find yourself questioning your path, the reasons behind your pursuits, and even your role in chasing these dreams. As a Black teen, you will also face external challenges—societal stereotypes and misconceptions about who you are and what you represent. These biases can come from others who, knowingly or unknowingly, cast doubts on your intentions or even view you as a threat to existing norms and institutions.

In the face of these challenges, it's crucial to have tools that help you maintain focus and stay grounded in your truth. One such powerful tool is affirmations. They are not just words but a transformative force that can continuously validate your identity and your aspirations. They act as a personal anchor, helping you navigate through negativity and stay aligned with your goals.

Let's delve into some real-life scenarios where affirmations have played a pivotal role in increasing ambition and steadying the road to someone's future. These examples will not only illustrate the power of affirmations but also provide you with practical insights on how to apply them in your own life.

Scenario: Embracing the Challenge in the Debate Club

First-Person Perspective: Ever since I can remember, the dynamic world of debate and politics, and the profound impact they wield have captivated me. Thriving in my high school debate club, I eagerly joined the university debate team, anticipating a continuation of my passion. However, the reality was starkly different. As I attended the first few sessions, it became evident that my peers were leagues ahead. They fluently referenced historical dates, quoted renowned philosophers, and navigated complex political theories with ease. Amid their eloquence and knowledge, I felt out of my depth, realizing that my understanding was somewhat rudimentary. This knowledge gap sparked doubts about my abilities and place in the debate club.

Effect on Belief System: The initial excitement of joining the university debate team quickly gave way to a sense of inadequacy. At each meeting, as I struggled to keep pace with discussions, I felt increasingly alienated and questioned my suitability for the debate world. The more I compared myself to my peers, the more my confidence eroded, leaving me to wonder if my passion for debate was misplaced.

Positive Affirmations:

- "I am on my own unique journey of learning and growth in debate."
- "Every expert was once a beginner, and I am embracing my path to expertise."
- "I bring a fresh perspective and valuable insights to every discussion, even as I learn."
- "My passion for debate is valid, and my knowledge will expand with each experience."

Reaffirmed Belief System: The transformative power of these affirmations became evident in my approach to participating in the debate club. Instead of being daunted by what I did not know, I focused on the opportunities for learning and growth each session offered. Recognizing that expertise is a journey, I began to value my unique perspectives and contributions, understanding that they add depth to discussions. This shift rebuilt my confidence and reignited my passion for debate. I actively participated, bravely posed questions, and valued the information others shared, viewing it as a guide for my personal growth.

These affirmations reinforced that my journey in debate is not defined by immediate expertise but by continuous growth and the courage to engage and learn. Embracing this has allowed me to thrive in the debate club, turning what initially felt like insurmountable challenges into stepping stones toward becoming a knowledgeable and confident debater.

Scenario: Charting My Own Course in Music

First-Person Perspective: Growing up, my father always envisioned a career in engineering for me, just like his. He frequently discusses the importance of Black individuals entering high-level industry roles early in life, concerned that too many are distracted by the glamorous lifestyles portrayed on TV. While he pushes for academic excellence and athletic involvement, my passion lies elsewhere. I've been playing guitar for six years, a hobby I've fallen deeply in love with, growing more dedicated and skilled over time. However, my father seems oblivious to my musical achievements, focusing instead on my grades and sports, particularly basketball, which I've lost interest in. The thought of confronting him about quitting basketball in favor of music terrifies me. I know the odds are tough, and I'm realistic about needing a backup plan, but music is where my heart truly lies.

Effect on Belief System: My father's constant emphasis on engineering and sports has instilled a deep fear of rejection and misunderstanding about my true aspirations. This fear has made me question my own dreams, causing me to wonder if pursuing music is just a fanciful escape rather than a legitimate career path. The pressure to conform to his expectations weighs heavily on me, dampening my enthusiasm and self-confidence in my musical talents.

Positive Affirmations:

- "I am entitled to pursue my passions and craft my future."
- "My dreams are valid, and my creative talents are worth pursuing."
- "I communicate my desires and plans confidently, deserving respect and understanding."
- "I am prepared to navigate challenges and remain committed to my goals."

Reaffirmed Belief System: Armed with these affirmations, I began to reshape how I viewed my conversation with my father. Instead of fearing his reaction, I focused on expressing my passion for music and my plan to responsibly pursue it alongside a practical backup. These affirmations helped me realize that my journey is my own to determine, and while his approval is important, my fulfillment is paramount. They bolstered my courage to finally have the conversation, presenting my aspirations not as mere whims but as serious and thought-out plans.

Outcome: When I spoke to my father, armed with clarity and confidence from my affirmations, the discussion was more constructive than I anticipated. While he had reservations, he could see my commitment and passion. This dialogue has started to bridge our understanding, and while it's an ongoing conversation, I feel more empowered and supported to pursue a path that truly resonates with me.

These affirmations continue to reinforce my resolve and confidence in forging my own path in music.

Here's how you can integrate affirmations into your daily life to reinforce your belief in yourself and your dreams:

1. **"I define my path and my success. I am driven by my aspirations, not by the doubts of others."** Use this affirmation to remind yourself that your goals and dreams are valid and that your journey is defined by your choices, not external opinions.

2. **"I am resilient, strong, and capable. My potential is limitless, and I pursue my dreams with courage."** This affirmation helps to bolster your confidence and reminds you of your inherent strength and ability to overcome obstacles.

3. **"My heritage is my strength. I draw power from my roots, and it propels me toward my future."** Embrace this affirmation to honor and draw strength from your cultural heritage, seeing it as a unique force that enhances your journey.

4. **"I am a positive influence. I inspire those around me with my effort and dedication."** Affirm your role as a leader and a positive example in your community, emphasizing how your actions can inspire and uplift others.

5. **"Setbacks are stepping stones. I learn from each experience and grow stronger in my resolve."** Resilience is promoted by this statement, as it presents difficulties as chances for development and education rather than hindrances.

By reciting these affirmations as part of a daily routine, you create a mindset that is steady, strong, and focused on pursuing big dreams. They serve not only as personal declarations of your intentions and values, but also as constant reminders that you are more than capable of achieving greatness.

It is crucial to personalize these affirmations, as they are only as effective as they are relevant to you. To make them a foundation, ensure that you believe them sincerely and say them regularly.

EMBRACING FAILURES AS A PART OF GROWTH

Mistakes, poor planning, and uninformed decisions pave the way for every journey toward success. To leverage these experiences, the first step is to accept your humanity and its role in your growth and evolution. We learn actively from our mistakes as individuals; without them, we do not evolve or improve in meaningful ways. Recognizing failure as a stepping stone toward growth and achievement is an essential mindset for anyone on a path to success.

Reframing Failures as Lessons for Growth

Viewing your failures not as setbacks but as invaluable lessons for personal and professional growth is crucial. Each time you make a mistake or fall short of a goal, you gain insights into what went wrong and how you can improve. This perspective turns each failure into a stepping stone toward future success.

When you don't achieve your desired outcome, reflect on the experience to extract lessons and apply them moving forward. This process of reflection and adaptation is vital, as it prevents the recurrence of similar mistakes and enhances your problem-solving skills. Recognizing these experiences as valuable lessons encourages a mindset of continuous learning and resilience.

Instead of harboring feelings of shame about your failures, embrace them as critical milestones on your journey. Each misstep provides a more precise direction for your subsequent efforts and strengthens your resolve. By acknowledging and analyzing your failures, you transform them into foundations for success.

Embracing this perspective requires a shift from viewing failures as endpoints to seeing them as integral parts of your growth narrative. This shift cultivates resilience and equips you with the knowledge from past experiences to take bold steps towards achieving your ambitions.

Fostering Resilience to the Impact of Failures

Having the ability to bounce back after setbacks is crucial for individuals striving to attain their objectives. Cultivating resilience entails learning to swiftly recover from setbacks and avoid excessive discouragement. Failures are a recurring part of life's journey; each is different and comes with its share of emotional weight. It's perfectly normal to experience disappointment or discouragement when things don't go as planned. However, it's crucial to prevent these feelings from stalling your progress.

Establish a proactive plan for coping with potential setbacks to effectively manage the impact of failures. This plan should include maintaining open communication with friends and family, who can offer support and perspective when you need it most. By sharing your challenges, you lighten your emotional load and reinforce your social support network, which is vital for resilience.

Furthermore, use your failure experiences to learn valuable lessons. Examine what went wrong and consider what you could do differently in the future. This reflective process turns setbacks into learning opportunities, providing critical insights that foster personal and professional growth. Instead of allowing failures to diminish your spirit, let them serve as motivation to push forward.

Affirmations like "I learn and grow from every experience," "I am capable of overcoming any challenge," and "Every setback is a setup for a comeback" can help reframe your perspective on failure. They encourage a focus on growth and progress, even in the face of difficulties.

By embracing these strategies, you cultivate resilience that helps you bounce back from failures and propels you towards future successes.

Maintaining Motivation Amid Setbacks

Maintaining motivation in the face of setbacks is crucial for sustained success. It's about sticking to your routines and keeping your focus sharp, even when faced with disappointments. When a project fails, or you encounter an unexpected hurdle, it's easy to feel discouraged. However, it's essential to engage in self-reflection during these moments. Review the steps you took, analyze the outcomes, and remind yourself that failure is an integral part of learning and growth.

To keep your motivation alive, consistently remind yourself of the bigger picture and the goals you are working towards. Understand that the path to success is rarely a straight line; it often includes detours and roadblocks. When your journey seems to stall, remember that it's within your power to reignite your momentum. By actively choosing to move forward, you signal to yourself that progress is still possible.

Here are a few strategies to help maintain your motivation:

- **Set Clear, Achievable Goals:** Break down your larger objectives into smaller, manageable tasks that can give you a sense of accomplishment regularly.
- **Celebrate Small Wins:** Every step forward deserves recognition. Celebrating the smallest victories can boost your morale and keep you motivated to keep pushing forward.
- **Stay Connected with Your Why:** Regularly remind yourself why you started on this path in the first place. Reconnecting with your initial motivations can provide a fresh surge of energy.
- **Seek Feedback and Support:** Don't isolate yourself. Reach out to mentors, peers, or supportive friends who can offer constructive feedback and encouragement.

- **Adjust Your Strategies as Needed:** Be flexible in your approach. If certain strategies aren't working, be willing to adapt and try new methods that yield better results.

Remember, the effort to maintain motivation is continuous. Just like sailing, you may need to adjust your sails, change direction, or weather a storm. But with persistence and a proactive attitude, the winds of opportunity will pick up, propelling you toward your aspirations.

Staying on Your Feet: Transforming Setbacks Into Stepping Stones

This section celebrates the resilience and determination of individuals and groups who turned significant setbacks into profound learning opportunities, catalyzing substantial change. Here, we explore the inspiring stories of those who faced daunting challenges yet used these moments not as deterrents but as springboards for growth and innovation. These narratives not only highlight the power of perseverance but also illustrate how adversity can be a critical component of success. Let's delve into the lives of remarkable people and movements that transformed their struggles into triumphs, shaping their paths and influencing the world.

Kai Bond: Kai Bond, a partner at Courtside VC, navigated the highly competitive and challenging venture capital industry as a Black professional. In an industry where Black individuals are significantly underrepresented, Bond faced numerous obstacles. Despite these challenges, he has made noteworthy strides in tech, co-founding a venture capital firm. Bond's journey is a testament to turning professional hurdles into stepping stones for success and breaking barriers within traditionally exclusive sectors.

The Black Panther Party: In 1966, the Black Panther Party took a stand against systemic racism and police brutality in Oakland, California, despite facing intense opposition. Despite government pushback and public misrepresentation, the party leveraged their setbacks as catalysts for community organization and social change. They established influential community service programs, including free breakfast programs for children, health clinics, and education initiatives. These programs supported low-income Black communities and highlighted the potential for grassroots movements to institute societal reforms.

Frederick Douglass: Frederick Douglass, born into slavery, faced unimaginable hardships early in his life. However, his relentless pursuit of education and freedom began an illustrious career as an abolitionist, writer, and orator. Douglass used his personal experiences with oppression to fuel his fight for the abolition of slavery and, later, for the suffrage of all disenfranchised populations. His ability to turn personal trials into a force for widespread societal change remains one of the most inspiring stories in American history.

What Can We Learn?

These stories are a testament to the resilience of the human spirit. They show us how setbacks can be transformed into powerful lessons and catalysts for change. Each of these figures or groups used their challenges not only to propel their own aspirations but also to influence broader societal transformations. Their journeys highlight the importance of resilience, the power of education, and the impact of steadfast dedication to one's principles and goals.

Design Your Dream Blueprint

Let's do an exercise to help you visualize and plan your journey. Achieving your goals becomes easier when you can see them in front of you. Here are instructions for sketching your "Dream Blueprint." Clarify your goals and understand the necessary steps to reach them. Predict potential obstacles and create strategies to overcome them. With strategic planning, a deeper understanding of your direction, and a clear visual aid, you'll strengthen your resilience and determination.

How to Create Your Dream Blueprint:

1. Set Your Aspirations:

- **Define Your Dreams:** What are the big goals you aim to achieve? These could span various aspects of your life, such as career, education, personal growth, or creative endeavors. Write them down as the starting points of your blueprint.

2. Detail the Steps:

- **Actionable Steps:** Break down each goal into tangible, achievable steps. Outline what you need to do first, what comes next, and so on, creating a flow of activities leading to your ultimate objectives.

3. Identify Obstacles:

- **Predict Challenges:** Think ahead about the challenges you might face. These could include external barriers like resource limitations or internal conflicts such as self-doubt.

4. Strategize Overcoming Obstacles:

- **Solution Strategies:** For each challenge identified, devise a strategy to overcome it. This might involve seeking additional resources, enhancing your skills, or adjusting your timelines.

5. Visualization and Reflection:

- **Draw Your Blueprint:** Use a large sheet of paper or a digital tool to visually map out your blueprint. Start with your end goals at the top and branch out to include steps, obstacles, and strategies.
- **Reflective Questions:** Contemplate questions such as what drives you to these goals, how achieving them would impact your life and the lives of others, and what resources you need to gather to propel you on this journey.

6. Regular Review and Adaptation:

- **Dynamic Planning:** Your Dream Blueprint should be a dynamic tool—regularly review and adapt it as you progress in your journey. It is updated as you complete steps, encounter new challenges, or even discover new aspirations.

By visualizing your goals and outlining a clear path to achieve them, you create a powerful tool for focus and motivation. This blueprint will serve as a constant reminder of where you want to go and how you can get there.

Final Thoughts

As we conclude our journey together, remember that the power of affirmations is not just about declaring your goals —it's about fueling the belief that you can achieve them. This final chapter has reinforced the significance of maintaining ambition and self-belief, particularly for Black youth who, like you, are striving to turn dreams into reality. Your resilience and determination are your greatest assets, and they will carry you far.

Your path to success is a journey of continuous growth and learning. Like the stories of Bessie Coleman, Kai Bond, and the Black Panther Party, your journey will include its fair share of challenges and setbacks. However, the lessons learned from these icons of resilience and determination underscore a vital truth: stumbling is a part of the human experience, but the courage to rise and persist defines true success.

Embrace the tools and knowledge this book shares to transform your stumbles into stepping stones. Build resilience against failures and learn to view them not as barriers but as opportunities to grow stronger and wiser. Remember, your journey isn't solitary. You are part of a community that cheers for your victories and extends a helping hand when challenges arise. Your community is here for you, always.

Keep your affirmations close and your community closer. With these in your arsenal, you are unstoppable. As we conclude this book, we'll reflect on the overarching lessons and discuss proactive steps to carry forward the momentum you've built. Let's look ahead and envision a future where you stand empowered, equipped, and ever-inspired to pursue greatness.

Ready to Inspire?

The future is yours for the taking. There will be challenges ahead, but you're ready to face them, and as you step forward with determination, remember that you can help others to get there too. In fact, you can start right now!

Simply by sharing your honest opinion of this book and a little about your own experience, you'll inspire more young Black men like you to become the master of their own destiny.

LET'S HEAR FROM YOU!

Thank you so much for your support. You're at the start of a huge adventure: Make sure it's an amazing one.

Scan the QR code below

CONCLUSION

As we conclude this enlightening journey, let's reflect on the true essence of what we have uncovered. This book was crafted not just to educate but to empower you, particularly as a young Black male, to harness the transformative power of affirmations. These tools are not merely words, but seeds planted deep within your psyche, designed to grow into pillars of strength and resilience. They don't cost you anything; you only have something to gain by trying them out. We've explored the science that backs them and supplied testimonials and success stories that backed their potentially life-changing effects. Affirmations are a potent force for personal and community empowerment. They are the chorus of your life's soundtrack, reminding you of your inherent worth, potential, and capability to effect change. By embracing and practicing daily affirmations, you're improving your own life and setting a foundation to uplift your community.

We've seen the power of a positive mindset exemplified by figures like Bessie Coleman and Martin Luther King Jr., whose lives remind us that any barrier can be overcome with determination and a strong belief in oneself. These stories underline the book's central takeaways, such as believing in yourself, embracing your community, and turning challenges into opportunities.

Holding your ground with poise and purpose becomes essential in a world often shadowed by stereotypes and opposition. This book has armed you with affirmations and mindfulness techniques that fortify your emotional resilience, enabling you to navigate through challenges with a steady mind. These tools don't just shield you against negativity; they open your eyes to diverse perspectives while guarding you against unfounded doubts and biases.

Throughout these pages, you've discovered the integral steps to becoming a leader—one who respects themselves and their community. Leadership may seem daunting initially, but equipped with the right affirmations and an unwavering spirit; you will be confident enough to guide others with dignity and grace. Remember, leaders are not merely born but forged through relentless effort and a humble acceptance of their imperfections.

As you put down this book and step into your daily life, remember that each new day is a blank slate, a fresh opportunity to paint your life with the colors of your strengths, dreams, and affirmations. Morning rituals, such as affirming your worth and potential, can ignite a powerful shift within you. These are not just words; they are catalysts for action, reinforcing your commitment to personal growth and your influence in the world.

Make a commitment to yourself to engage in daily affirmations. Whether it's stating, "I am capable of overcoming any obstacle," or "I am a leader in my community," these affirmations are the roots that ground your spirit and the wings that propel your dreams. They mold your reality by reshaping your thoughts, which in turn transform your actions and, ultimately, your life's trajectory.

The path may not always be smooth, but it's paved with invaluable lessons that forge your strength and character. Throughout this book, we've explored various strategies— from understanding the power of language in shaping our identity, as discussed by Daniel Everett, to the neurological impacts of self-affirmation studied by researchers like Cascio et al.

As you move forward, apply the principles of goal-setting and affirmations discussed here to various aspects of your life, whether it's your academic pursuits, career ambitions, or personal relationships. Embrace the practice of creating vision boards as a tangible representation of your aspirations and a daily reminder of where you are headed.

Additionally, the cultivation of healthy relationships and the art of effective communication are crucial for your personal and professional growth. These are not just skills but are essential components of a supportive network that will uplift you throughout your journey.

Remember, your story is one of continual growth and discovery. Each challenge you encounter is not a setback but an opportunity to learn, adapt, and emerge stronger. Your daily affirmations are your armor and strength, fortifying your resolve and reminding you of your intrinsic worth and potential.

Start each day with a clear vision of your goals, maintain the resilience to pursue them, and let your life be a testament to the power of self-belief and persistent effort.

Let this book be the beginning, not the end, of your journey to a life filled with success, happiness, and positive impact. As we close this chapter, look forward with excitement to the following steps on your path, knowing you are equipped and ready to create a future that reflects your highest aspirations.

REFERENCES

ASVAB Career Exploration Program. (n.d.). Asvab program. Retrieved April 27, 2024, from https://www.asvabprogram.com/media-center-article/65

Biggers, A., Spears, C. A., Sanders, K., Ong, J., Sharp, L. K., & Gerber, B. S. (2020). Promoting Mindfulness in African American Communities. *Mindfulness, 11*(10), 2274–2282. https://doi.org/10.1007/s12671-020-01480-w

Biron, A. (2022, February 13). *Black History in the making: 10 young leaders on the rise.* Manchester Ink Link. https://manchesterinklink.com/black-history-in-the-making-10-young-leaders-on-the-rise/

Cascio, C. N., O'Donnell, M. B., Tinney, F. J., Lieberman, M. D., Taylor, S. E., Strecher, V. J., & Falk, E. B. (2015). Self-affirmation activates brain systems associated with self-related processing and reward and is reinforced by future orientation. *Social Cognitive and Affective Neuroscience, 11*(4), 621–629. https://doi.org/10.1093/scan/nsv136

Celebrating Some of the Most Influential African American Leaders. (2022, February 2). NSLS. https://www.nsls.org/blog/african-american-leaders-in-history

Deaderick, L. (2023, December 23). *Nonprofit "Mentor of the Year" uses example of an early mentor, his aunt, in his work.* San Diego Union-Tribune. https://www.sandiegouniontribune.com/lifestyle/people/story/2023-12-23/nonprofit-mentor-of-the-year-uses-example-of-an-early-mentor-his-aunt-in-his-work

DeAngelis, T. (2014, October). *Building resilience among black boys.* APA. *https://www.apa.org/monitor/2014/10/cover-resilience*

Effects of Stereotypes on Personal Development. (2022, November 16). Quebec.ca. https://www.quebec.ca/en/family-and-support-for-individuals/childhood/child-development/effects-stereotypes-personal-development/definition-stereotypes

8 Young Black Trailblazers To Support in 2023! (2023, February 1). *8 Young Black Trailblazers To Support in 2023!* Channel Kindness. https://www.channelkindness.org/8-black-trailblazers-2023/

Hanscom, D. (2020, January 30). *Affirmations and Neuroplasticity.* Psychology

Today. https://www.psychologytoday.com/us/blog/anxiety-another-name-pain/202001/affirmations-and-neuroplasticity

Harris, M. (2019, September 26). *Positive Relationships Boost Self-Esteem, and Vice Versa.* APA. https://www.apa.org/news/press/releases/2019/09/relationships-self-esteem

Havens, R. (n.d.). *10 Influential Figures to Celebrate During Black History Month.* Unexpected Virtual Tours. Retrieved April 27, 2024, from https://unexpectedvirtualtours.com/resources/influential-black-figures/

Kindelan, K. (2021, February 16). *Black Girls Breathing founder shares tips to use your breath to help ease stress.* Good Morning America. https://www.goodmorningamerica.com/wellness/story/black-girls-breathing-founder-shares-tips-breath-ease-75893231

Knorr, E. (2020, July 14). *Being Black in IT: 3 tech leaders share their stories.* CIO. https://www.cio.com/article/193711/being-black-in-it-3-tech-leaders-share-their-stories.html

Kurin, R. (2022, February 22). *Because It Can Help Preserve Cultural Heritage Important for Understanding and Social Benefit.* Why Social Science? https://www.whysocialscience.com/blog/2022/2/22/because-it-can-help-preserve-cultural-heritage-important-for-understanding-and-social-benefit

Lee, D. S. (2023, March 2). *How Mentors Impact Youth in the Black Community.* Forward Together Colorado. https://parents.forwardtogeth erco.com/how-mentors-impact-youth-in-the-black-community/

Leonard, Michael. *4 Thought Provoking Will Smith Quotes on the Law of Attraction.* Fearless Soul - Inspirational Music & Life Changing Thoughts, 25 April 2018. https://iamfearlesssoul.com/will-smith-quotes-law-attraction/

Martin Luther King Quote Analysis - 897 Words. (n.d.). Internet Public Library. https://www.ipl.org/essay/Martin-Luther-King-Quote-Analysis-F33CSBWMG5PT

Metcalf, M. (n.d.). *Can you imagine your way to success? It's possible. These six techniques for visualization are a great place to start.* Getmarlee. Retrieved April 27, 2024, from https://getmarlee.com/blog/visualization

Moore, C. (2019, March 4). *Positive Daily Affirmations: Is There Science Behind It?* PositivePsychology.com. https://positivepsychology.com/daily-affirmations/

The Black Panther Party: Challenging Police and Promoting Social Change. (n.d.). National Museum of African American History & Culture. https://

nmaahc.si.edu/explore/stories/black-panther-party-challenging-police-and-promoting-social-change

Trent, N. (2018). *Frederick Douglass | Biography, Life, & Facts*. Encyclopædia Britannica. https://www.britannica.com/biography/Frederick-Douglass

Williams, A. (2015, July 8). *8 successful people who use the power of visualization*. Mindbodygreen. https://www.mindbodygreen.com/arti cles/successful-people-who-use-the-power-of-visualization

Zagada, M. (2020, March 13). *More Than Words: How Language Affects The Way We Think*. GoFLUENT | United States. https://www.gofluent.com/ us-en/blog/how-language-affects-the-way-we-think/

Made in the USA
Las Vegas, NV
16 October 2024

97013170R00105